3rd Generation Country

3rd Generation Country

A Practical Guide to Raising Children with Great Values

BeNeca Ward

To order additional copies of this book, contact:
Xlibris Corporation
1-888-795-4274
www.Xlibris.com
Orders@Xlibris.com
66084

ACKNOWLEDGEMENTS

I have to first thank **GOD** for giving me the vision, time and strength to write this book. The experience has been such a Blessing.

This book is dedicated to **my mother** whose words of wisdom have always stayed on my mind. Thank you. Your love is much appreciated. I hope that my daughters gain as much knowledge from me as I did from you.

Aaliyah and Alani-Mommy thanks you for the patience that you have had through this process. I so love and appreciate the gift of who you two are and the flowers that you continue to be in my life.

Daddy-thank you for all of your encouragement and the late night conference calls with your friends about your own "3rd Generation Country" stories. You really helped me with my process. **Sukari, Destini, Dynysty, India & Asia**—thank you for being the best sisters and a wonderful support system who pushed me forward when I was tired and watched the girls when I needed a break so that I could make it to the finish line. **Shawond**—thank you for holding my hand through conversations that reminded me that I would make it all the way through the process regardless of what was going on around me. For that I am grateful. **Papa Stan**—thank you for allowing me to be "3rd Generation Country" in my every day over the past almost 20 years. Your guidance, love and support have been embedded in to who I am today. **Aunt Gloria**—thank you for taking your time with me as a child and filling my mind with such great memories. **Vanessa**—you were the first person who knew about this book. Thank you for making me sit down and start writing out the vision and encouraging me on along the way. **Dawn**—I thank GOD for our many phone calls that lead me past my "Street Signs to Victory" and kept my perspective focused on the things in life that are truly important. **Do Re Me Learning Center, Carla C., Aunt Bea, Grandpa, Briggette, Carla L, Janice, Rikki & Amber**—thank you for your love and support. **Nicole**—thank you for being my "Mirrored Image" through this process. **Kenisha & Cia**—thanks for giving me a fresh place to think, write, vent and relax. **Kristen, Annya, Rhonda, Dilini, Crystal and my SLMG Family**-thanks for taking the time to read this in the early stages and sharing your thoughts. **Kelly**—thank you for being my cheering squad and bringing clarity to the vision. To all of my family and friends who have supported me through this journey, I thank you very much.

TABLE OF CONTENTS

INTRODUCTION

As I entered my adult years, when asked why I did something in such a particular way when it came to my values and practices, I'd always say it was because I was "third-generation country." My grandmother, born in the 1920s, was considered "first-generation country" because she was a part of the first generation that helped to set the American standards on family structure and raising children with great values. My mother, born in the 1950s, helped carry the torch on to the second generation. The fact that I was born my mother's child in the 1970s earned me the title of third-generation country.

This book focuses on the values and practices that were instilled into American children for at least three generations but for many reasons are no longer being taught. Years ago, parents passed on to their children the lessons that they learned as children while stirring in life experiences that related to what was going on in the world as their children were growing up. This book was written because I noticed that there were so many things that we (my generation) were taught about life just from everyday living that were not passed on to the generation that came after ours or the children that came after them. Although our parents took the time to talk to us, they rarely had time to sit us down and explain the ways in which all the pieces of the puzzle of life fit together. Instead, they gave us bits and pieces of life firsthand that helped us to put the puzzle together ourselves. This is a reminder for some and a guide for others on how to raise children using the practical lessons of yesterday that are being forgotten and/or thrown away because times are changing. Even though times are changing, how we raise our children and the lessons that we allow them to learn firsthand should not. It's similar to the difference between "on-the-job training" (how we were raised) and "learning from books on tape" (telling children everything because we think that they are too young or not capable of learning on their own even when using the simplest methods). This book will make you laugh as you reflect upon your own experiences and are tuned in to the experiences of others. It will also make you realize how much was once taught through the simplest lessons. As my mother was reading through this, she asked me how I was able to get so much from what seemed to be so little. She discovered that although I didn't always seem to be listening, through her direction, she had taught me how to truly pay attention. Because all children are different, they need to be loved, given a sense of structure, and disciplined in a way that works best for them based on their individual personality and circumstances. However, there are some basic practices that can be used with most children to help mold them into kind, respectful, and responsible adults.

CHAPTER ONE

Because I Said So

Because I Said So

This chapter is full of lessons that were taught to us as children through mere sayings, which subsequently helped us to grow into respectful adults who are mindful of others.

SAYINGS USED:

Respect your Elders.

Stay out of Grown Folks Business.

What happens at our house stays at our house.

Because I said so.

Talking out of turn, also known as Backtalk

Know your place.

Mind your own business-You should have enough of your own.

I am not one of your little friends.

Don't let your company get you into trouble.

Be careful about the company that you keep.

I know you're not acting out.

But what did *I* tell you to do?

What did I tell you last?

Use your common sense.

Almost everything you have is mine.

ONE

The saying "Respect is earned," although very valid in many circumstances, has been taken too far out of context, especially as it pertains to children. We were taught that respect should be given to whomever we met, when we met them, unless we were given a reason not to do so. When visiting an elementary school one day, I was amazed to hear the children call the teachers by their first names. Although I saw who they were talking to, I still wanted to believe that there was a child nearby with the exact same name. One day, upon my arrival, a little girl, who seemed to be very upset and confused, approached me and asked, "How come your daughters have to say Mr. and Ms. before all the adults' names?" I turned around and simply said, "Honey, it is because it shows respect." She looked at me as though she had no idea what the word *respect* meant and said, "Okay." I found that to be so interesting because when I was in school, it was a big deal if we even *knew* our teachers' first names. I remember kids saying to one another, "Guess what, guess what? I found out that Ms. Johnson's real name is Shirley," implying that *Ms. Johnson* was a title that had been given to her. This title was something royal-like that required that we respected her. It made us pay attention to her when she spoke and helped us to understand that we could learn a lot from her because she was at a different level *in life* than we were and knew more than we did. There was something about just calling her Shirley that would have put us all on the same level. When I was growing up, all children addressed every adult by title. Whether it was Mr. or Ms., Mom, Dad, Grandma, Grandpa, Auntie, or Uncle, if they were grown and we were not, they had their own special title. Family friends who were too close to us to be called Mr. or Ms. but weren't really related to us often became an honorary aunt or uncle. Aside from these titles, there was also an "older cousin" rule that applied to any cousin who was fifteen years or more our senior. Instead of saying "Betty," we addressed her as Cousin Betty. However, if she was twenty years older or more than we were, she was just considered to be our Auntie Betty because we were not viewed as being grown enough to be that casual with someone who was that much older than we were. For me, it instilled a sense of respect for people who were older and wiser than I was. I once met someone who said that she preferred that her toddler call adults by their first names because she did not want him to feel as though he was not on the same level as the adults. However, the reality is that A CHILD IS NOT ON THE SAME LEVEL AS AN ADULT. He or she is a child that has a lot to learn.

We were taught to respect everyone, especially those who were older and wiser than we were from whom we could learn. Children who are allowed to question their parents' every decision, debate with them on every topic, and are made to feel that they are on the same level in life, sometimes find it harder to see and understand that there is a real difference between themselves and their parents. Many are being led to believe that they were born with an educated opinion about everything. This way of thinking can prevent them from realizing how much they need to learn and is naturally why many children today have no respect for adults. We learned that no one graduates from elementary school with a master's or PhD.

SAYING USED: "RESPECT YOUR ELDERS"

When I was young, there was something called grown folks' business. Anytime there was a conversation or situation happening around us that only pertained to adult like matters and we, as children, felt the need to add our comments or questions, we were quickly reminded to "stay out of grown folks' business." Our parents chose not to discuss issues like overdue bills or unwanted pregnancies with us at an early age. They knew that those conversations would lead us out of our innocence as children and into the concerns of adults. They also realized that if we were given the opportunity to participate in those conversations, we would have questions about the subjects but not truly be able to understand the answers. The expression "Stay out of grown folks' business" was also used at times when our parents felt that it was not necessary for them to go further into detail about an explanation that they had just given to us. I remember asking my mother once to buy something for me, and she turned around and calmly said no, gave no real explanation, and then continued with her conversation about something else. For some crazy reason at that moment, even though I realized that she did hear and clearly understood my question, I still felt that I needed more clarification and began questioning her decision. After I continued to push the issue further on why she would not buy it, she reminded me that she did not owe me an explanation for her every decision. She went on to tell me that she was a grown woman who was very capable of making solid decisions without first consulting with an eight-year-old child. Although we were taught to think for ourselves and ask questions about the things that we did not understand, we were also taught not to question our parents when they gave us a final answer but to trust in their decisions.

The phrase "stay out of grown folks' business" was used as a quick reminder that taught us that it was not okay to question our parents about everything. It kept us from being stressed out by the troubles that adults were faced with, helped us to maintain our innocence for as long as possible, and reminded us to step back into our place as children.

SAYING USED: "STAY OUT OF GROWN FOLKS' BUSINESS"

"What happens at our house stays at our house" was a phrase used to prevent any conversation that may have slipped through the cracks of "stay out of grown folks' business" from being shared with other people outside of our home. How my mother chose to work out the kinks of our household troubles was not something that she wanted made known to our neighbors, teachers, friends, or even other family members. She felt that if it wasn't something that directly affected them that they did not need to be involved. This phrase helped prevent "family business" (e.g., what someone's mother was really thinking about their father or who got into trouble the night before) from being publicized when some child thought that they were grown enough to have grown folks' conversations outside of their parents' home. We would have serious consequences to deal with if our parents found out that we were outside gossiping about and/or embarrassing one of our family members. They felt that it was important that we were allowed to go through certain issues and learn certain lessons within the privacy of our own home.

This reminded us that certain things are to be kept private and not meant for all to hear. It also taught us to always make sure that all of our conversations are not only appropriate but also necessary.

SAYING USED: "WHAT HAPPENS AT OUR HOUSE STAYS AT OUR HOUSE"

When I was a little girl, "Because I said so" was a common phrase that was the end-all and be-all of an entire conversation (short for "This is the end of all your questions" and "that will be all for now"). It was usually something that was said to us after we were given an explanation that we did not want to hear or if there was no time for someone to further explain a situation that was happening right in front of us. My mom taught us, through example, that we could trust whatever she said or whatever decision she made, and that if she could not thoroughly explain a situation to us at that time, we would eventually, over time, understand it. It seems to be the norm these days for kids to ask the same questions over and over or go into a tantrum and use words like *frustrated* if they do not hear the answer that they would like to hear. It's funny because when I was growing up, we weren't allowed to use words like *frustrated* until we had a job and were able to support ourselves. Because roles in relationships have to be established first and then worked on from within, our parents established that they were the parents in our relationship and explained to us exactly what that meant. We would often be given information at their discretion or what used to be referred to as information on a need-to-know basis. Today, when parents are answering *to* their child, the answer "Because I said so" cannot be used nor will it be respected.

Because we learned to trust our parents early on, we grew to understand that they would make the decision that they thought was best.

SAYING USED: "BECAUSE I SAID SO"

Talking out of turn, often referred to as back talk, was never an option in our home. The phrase "talking out of turn" means just what it says: talking when it's not your turn. When we were in trouble and my mother was talking to us, she did not allow us to interrupt her in the middle of her sentence because she knew that if we were talking while she was talking, we could not have possibly been listening to what she was saying. The fact that I was not allowed to talk back to my parents and was required to wait until they finished speaking or asking their question at hand before I could respond forced me to increase my listening skills over time. It also taught me that whenever I am in a situation where I have done something wrong, I should always listen to what the other person involved has to say first and then respond rather than just responding out of emotion. Our society has taught parents to raise their children to have their own set of rules, the freedom of speech and expression in every situation and the belief that they would never be reprimanded for what they say. Although we learned how to form an opinion about our likes and dislikes we also knew how to figure out when it was appropriate to voice our opinion.

We were taught to understand that as adults, we would not be allowed to talk out of turn in places like our classrooms, work environments, and courtrooms.

SAYING USED: TALKING OUT OF TURN, ALSO KNOWN AS BACK TALK

At one point in time, it was common to hear adults remind children to know their place or know how to figure out what their role was supposed to be within whatever circumstance they were faced with. Understanding this concept drew a clear image that reminded us that we were not all that filled the frame of a picture but a specific piece within its beauty. It helped us learn how to adjust to any situation and made us be aware of our place in other people's business. It also taught us that our opinion was not always necessary, required, wanted, or appropriate. I remember walking into the room as my mother was telling a really funny story to one of her girlfriends. I entered the room toward the end of the joke and just fell out laughing. My mother stopped her laugh right in the middle and asked me, "What are *you* laughing at?" She asked the question as though my laugh did not qualify for her joke. When I looked back on the situation I realized that it didn't because it wasn't my place to be in her business.

This mind-set taught us that our place *is not in everyone's conversation, everyone's office, everyone's house, or everyone's business. It also taught us how to feel situations out by the vibe in the room and to respect other peoples' space. If we walked into a room and people were talking about matters that did not pertain to us, we learned how to excuse ourselves and come back at a more appropriate time.*

SAYING USED: "KNOW YOUR PLACE"

Whenever a kid was in the middle of getting fussed at and I decided to add my two cents worth of advice about what I thought about the situation while they were being scolded, I was reminded to mind my own business. My mother was quick to take me back to the fact that I needed to focus on all the things that were on my own to-do list. Whenever I took it upon myself to get into someone else's business, she always had a way of finding something that I was supposed to have had done but had not yet finished and would ask me how I could have had the time to worry about what someone else was doing when my homework was not finished or our room was not clean. "Mind your own business" was a saying that was commonly used to teach us that any situation that was happening in someone else's life that did not pertain to our own and we were not able to be of any help was not any of our concern or any of our business. My mom would ask questions like "How can you be a tattletale when you have not done what you are supposed to be doing?" or "Why are you paying so much attention to what somebody is doing? Don't you think that if you spent less time worrying about them, you would have more time to get your work done?" After being asked those questions so many times, we would often rather just keep whatever information that we had about someone else to ourselves so that our problems wouldn't be found out and revealed.

This lesson taught us that we should have enough going on in our own lives, and it should be so full that we do not have the time to talk about someone else's.

SAYING USED: "MIND YOUR OWN BUSINESS . . . YOU SHOULD HAVE ENOUGH OF YOUR OWN"

My mother's goal as a parent was never to be my friend but to always be my mother. She decided to focus on Proverbs 22:6 from the Bible that says, "Train a child in the way he should go, and when he is old he will not turn from it." She wanted to make sure that when we were out in the world, we knew right from wrong and conducted ourselves appropriately. She was not concerned with hanging out with us or crossing boundaries that would confuse her purpose in our lives. She wanted us to know, without a doubt, that when she spoke, it was something that we could learn from and trust. With all that she was determined to instill into who we would become, she had no time to focus on being our friend. Although my mom took the time to talk to us about what was going on in our lives and made sure that we felt good about ourselves, it was always understood when speaking to her that we were to treat her with a high level of respect. She would sometimes say, "I'm not one of your little friends." This was said to us as a reminder that there were specific things that we could not say to her, nor could we speak to her in the same tone of voice that we used when we were speaking to our friends. Many people try raising their children as their friends and this sometimes causes problems and creates a void where a child would normally be able to pull from in order to get what they need from their parent. We knew early on that we were not our parents' best friends. Since we had to stay out of grown folks' business, there was no way that they would ever consider us to be their best friend. We understood that we were their children and that they thought of us as just that, their children. Some parents today make their children their hangout buddies in an effort to make sure that they have company around for themselves. But as the kids get older and want to hang out with their own friends by themselves, there can sometimes be a cloud of guilt covering the child because of the "friendship" that has been created by the parent. It is one thing to make raising a child the first priority in a parent's life but something different when they make their child their entire life and never want them to leave. We were made to feel as though it was okay for us to move out and away from our parents' home once we were grown. It helped us to look forward to being responsible, independent adults. We really needed a parent, which for our parents was a job that had a purpose and a specific role in our lives. As I was growing up and times were starting to change, I noticed that my friends who needed parental advice but had only related to their parent as their friend, found someone else to talk to when they were specifically seeking "parental" advice. They often spoke to one of their friends' parents or another adult that they respected as a parental figure. This seemed to happen to those who had not been shown that their parents knew how to give solid advice or, as their friend, had always been full of answers like "What do you think?" and "It's up to you." This was not the response that we wanted to hear when we were already unsure about what to do in the situation that we were in. Even as teenagers, we knew that we needed to talk to someone who had the experience to guide us into the right direction. This is not to say that a true friendship cannot be developed between a parent and a child once they are both adults. However, there should always be a sense of respect for the parent within the tone of every conversation. Talking as friends and going back and forth with one's parents about something without any guidance along the way can be very confusing to a child. Once they become accustomed to voicing what they want, in the tone that they would use with their friends, they lose an understanding of where their boundaries should be within their relationship with their parents.

Although our parents were full of advice that we couldn't get away from as hard as we often tried, we learned that we could always trust their advice even though we did not always take it.

SAYING USED: "I AM NOT ONE OF YOUR LITTLE FRIENDS"

Because there was so much time invested into teaching us the differences between right and wrong, my mom was very adamant about making sure that we knew better than to let our friends influence us into doing the wrong things. Many parents used the phrase "Don't let your company (or friends) get you into trouble" as a way to encourage their kids to push past peer pressure. We were taught to understand that just because our friends were doing something wrong or going somewhere that they were not supposed to be going, it did not excuse us from doing the wrong thing. I learned that lesson the hard way in my last year of middle school when for some reason, my school decided to have our graduation the day before the last day of school. Most of our graduating class either stayed at home for the last day or met their friends at school and went somewhere else. One of my friends convinced me that I should leave school too and go with her back to her house for the day. She said that she would be glad to walk back with me when it was time for school to let out and that it would be okay because her mom was at home. She went on to tell me that nobody was at the school anyway, and because we already graduated, it didn't make much sense to stay. Unfortunately for me, I decided to listen to her and just as I was leaving the campus headed to her house, my school counselor saw me and quickly called my mother. She told her that she was so surprised to see me leave with the other girls and thought she should call her right away. She even went as far as to give her my friend's phone number and home address so that my mom could drive over there and pick me up. That was a day that I will never forget because after my mother picked me up, yelled at me for leaving the campus without her permission, and asked my friend's mom why she thought it was okay for me to be there without talking to her first, she then drove me back to the school, dropped me off to stay there for the rest of the day, and said, "Don't let your company get you into trouble." Our parents also used this phrase as a warning when they noticed or thought that our friends were doing something wrong and that we were about to make the same mistake.

This expression taught us and simply meant this: Do not let the company that you are keeping, better known as your friends, influence your decision to do something that you already know is going to get you into trouble.

SAYING USED: *"DON'T LET YOUR COMPANY GET YOU INTO TROUBLE"*

As teenagers, we quickly fell in love with our friends and always felt that they could do no wrong. However, our parents sometimes had a different opinion and viewpoint than we did about certain people. Whenever they were concerned about the motives of one of our friends based on something that they heard him or her say or saw him or her do, although they may not have stopped us from hanging out with that person right away, they would always pull us to the side and share the things that they had observed. One day, my mother was standing near one of my friends whom I just loved to pieces and overheard her say something about me that was not anything that a true friend would ever say. She looked at me directly in the eyes and said, "Honey, I know that she is your friend, and you like her a lot, but I would just like to tell you what I overheard her say." She went on to say, "I may be wrong about what she meant, but I want you to be careful about the company that you keep." We learned that the company that we keep or the people that we hang around with can greatly affect our lives and that their circumstances can easily become our own just by being at the wrong place at the wrong time. We also learned that one wrong decision can have a great effect on the rest of our lives. By the time we were teenagers, as long as our friends weren't drinking, smoking, being promiscuous, or skipping school, our parents allowed us to learn how to feel out certain situations and people for ourselves.

This was a lesson that pushed us to pay close attention to the actions of the people who we considered to be our friends. We learned to take notice on whether or not they had our best interest in mind and whether or not their decisions should be our own.

SAYING USED: "BE CAREFUL ABOUT THE COMPANY YOU KEEP"

The phrase "I know you are not acting out" was short for "I know you are not acting out of control or acting differently than how you have been raised to behave just because other people are around!" When we were younger, some of us thought that it would be easier to try out new behaviors in front of our parents when other people were nearby. It's kind of funny now to think back on how hard we tried to sneak things in just to get a reaction. Somehow we thought that if they didn't approve of what we were doing, we would not get into as much trouble because we knew how much they didn't like to be embarrassed in front of other people. What we found out was that before they would allow our actions to embarrass them, we would be embarrassed by the consequences. One of my most vivid memories relating to this was from something that happened one day when I asked my mom to take me to my friend's party. She initially told me that she was not going to be able to take me because she was not feeling well. Shortly afterward, she changed her mind but solely with the condition that I was only going to be able to stay at the party for a little while. I got so excited and said that I completely understood, but once we were there and she said that it was time for us to leave I started crying and begging to stay. Rather than losing her cool, she so calmly looked at me and said, "I know you're not acting out and do not want to be embarrassed in front of your friends." This immediately reminded me that I already knew what our original plan and agreement were. She took a moment to thank the parents, and we went on our way. But once we were in the car, she went on to say that because I proved that I was not able to understand what "a little while" meant, she would not be able to extend an offer like that one to me the next time that she didn't feel well.

This saying taught us a few different lessons. It reminded us that we should not forget the things that have been taught to us, we should never use our situation to manipulate our circumstances at someone else's expense, and we should always be on our best behavior no matter where we were or who was around.

SAYING USED: "I KNOW YOU'RE NOT ACTING OUT"

My mom was always very particular about whose care she left us under during the times when she could not be there. She tried to make sure that whoever was caring for us shared the same values and principles that she did and was always very specific when she gave us instructions, especially those that would apply when she was not around. Although we were raised to be respectful and mindful of what we said to adults, if someone told us that we could do something that we knew our mom had already told us we were not allowed to do, no matter who it was, she expected us to say "I am sorry, but I am not allowed to do that." If they were persistent about having us follow their rule instead of hers, she expected us to ask them to call her so that she could explain to them exactly what she meant. One day, she dropped us off at her friend's house for the evening. We didn't celebrate Halloween, and on this particular night, there was a Halloween carnival happening right down the street. The other children were all going to the carnival, and her friend insisted that we go too, telling us that she would explain the situation to my mother about how she told us that it was okay to go. In spite of the fact that her friend took the blame for all that had happened, at the end of the evening, we were still held accountable for what we knew we were supposed to say. The last thing that I remember my mother asking us was "But what did I tell you to do?"

Lessons like this reminded us to live by what we had been taught to do even when under pressure or in an unusual situation.

SAYING USED: "BUT WHAT DID I TELL YOU TO DO?"

"What did I tell you last?" and "What was the last thing that I told you to do?" were questions that pertained to the last set of instructions that our parents gave us about something specific that we were supposed to do. In spite of the first, second, or third set of directions that we might have been given, we were taught that we were to always do whatever they told us to do last. Over time, we learned that parents had the right to change their minds whenever they wanted to with no explanation needed. There were many occasions when we were told that we could do something like walk to the store with our friends, but just as we were about to walk out of the door, our parents changed their mind and said that we could not go. Every now and then, we would try to push the situation forward by saying something like "But you just told me that I could go," although the response would always be something like "Well, I changed my mind" or "What did I tell you last?" At first we thought that it was the craziest thing, and there were definitely times that we were given full explanations for answers that we had been given, but oftentimes we learned the hard way that our parents' decision to suddenly change our plans in the middle did not give us the right to question their reasoning.

This taught us to trust our parents and to understand that they did not need to explain themselves to us every time they changed their minds about a decision that they thought was best. This was very significant because it taught us how to listen and follow directions at the drop of a dime so that if there was ever an emergency and we were in a dangerous situation, we would know how to listen to and follow directions without asking a lot of questions, which could ultimately save our lives.

SAYING USED: "WHAT DID I TELL YOU LAST?"

Because our parents wanted us to learn how to think for ourselves, did not want to have to give us detailed instructions on what we were supposed to be doing all the time, and would sometimes only communicate through a firm look from across the room, we were often expected to figure things out based on what we knew to be fact or what we could assume depending on the circumstances that surrounded our situation. Basing our logic on the surrounding circumstances of a situation was often referred to as using common sense. It was crucial that we not only learned how to develop a certain amount of common sense but that we also learned how to use it as a tool. This at times helped us to read between the lines of certain things that were said to us and figure out what people were really trying to say in spite of what they might have actually said. So often our parents would tell us to do something like to clean off the kitchen counter. After we were finished, they'd come by and say "Good job, but how come you didn't sweep the floor when you finished?" If we said that it was because we were not told to do so, we would be asked why someone would have to tell us to sweep the floor if while cleaning the counter we dropped crumbs on the floor. They would go on to say that common sense should have told us to clean the floor. They expected common sense to tell us a whole lot of things. They'd say things like, "Common sense should have told you not to jump off of the top of that tree before you fell and broke your arm" or "Common sense should have told you that a man selling a TV, not in a box with no warranty, wasn't quite right." Common sense skills were also used as a gauge to let us know how cautious we needed to be when dealing with issues that involved our safety. If we ever found ourselves in a situation that made us feel uncomfortable, we were reminded to use our common sense or how we felt to determine whether or not we should leave right away.

This taught us that when we are putting effort toward doing anything, we should think about everything that will be required in order to complete the job and show initiative toward succeeding. It also taught us to be aware of our surroundings and always be in tune with what we feel inside.

SAYING USED: "USE YOUR COMMON SENSE"

Unlike many children today, we did not grow up having high levels of expectations or demands for our parents to fill nor were we allowed to carry a pocket full of entitlement. Although it was made very clear that our parents would do as much as they could do for us, they also made it very clear that everything that we had came from them or someone else other than ourselves and could therefore be returned if we became arrogant about "our things." When we decided to test them on this topic, we heard the speech that started with the sentences "Almost everything that you have is mine. I bought it. I just let you use, eat, or wear it." We were never allowed to be ornery but were reminded that because we did not have a job or provide for ourselves, certain privileges of being independent did not apply to us. It seemed to make my mother happy when she was able to provide us with certain things that we wanted. However, at the very moment that our attitude started to adjust in a negative direction, she would shine the light of reality onto us and remind us of our own reality.

This lesson taught us to be thankful and grateful for the things that other people were kind enough to provide for us. It also taught us as children that one day, if we worked hard, we would be able to provide the things that we wanted for ourselves.

SAYING USED: "ALMOST EVERYTHING YOU HAVE IS MINE"

CHAPTER TWO

The Patience of A Pomegranate

The Patience of A Pomegranate

This chapter reflects upon situations that taught us as children how to have patience. It also highlights certain circumstances that taught parents not only how to build up their level of patience but also how to exercise it while raising their children. From bringing a baby home from the hospital to teaching a child how to take one step at a time, there were many different lessons that contributed to building a solid amount of patience for both the parents and children.

PATIENCE LEARNED THROUGH:

Love and affection

Nurturing a baby at home

Avoiding nighttime air

Going the distance with and for your child

Waiting until our parents got home

Eating a pomegranate

Being "Neighborly" and helping others

Complaining about being bored

Staying where our parents could see us

Playing no farther than four houses down the street

Coming home before the street lights came on

Taking baby steps (walking, riding and driving)

The rules of school shopping

Putting clothes on Lay-Away

Allowing a child to become more independent during middle school years

Having a fifteen-minute time limit on the telephone

Waiting to have cell phone privileges

Waiting To Receive Something Until It Is Actually Needed

TWO

My parents saw the importance in expressing their love through hugs, kisses, tickles, and other playful gestures when their I-love-you was not being said out loud. Even after we had gotten into trouble or been put on punishment, they would still make a point to show us that they loved us through something as simple as a subtle glance from across the room, which was their way of saying "I love you even though you made a mistake." The love that they shared with us allowed us to see firsthand that it was okay to love someone with all our hearts. Our parents' patience and their decision to love us through our mistakes and beyond our tough times taught us to be forgiving and patient with those people who were around us. It helped us to be more open, honest, and up-front with them about the things that we did wrong, because we knew that regardless of the outcome, they would always be there by our side. It's funny because I remember someone in my family saying that she could fuss at her child and ask him if he wanted something to eat in the same sentence because the love that she had for him was not diminished based on what he was going through. Growing up, our parents' support was what initially made us more conscientious about making the right decisions because we did not want to disappoint them.

Our parents' love was on one hand an open door that kept us close to them during great times and on the other hand a closed door that prevented us from running away during trying times.

PATIENCE LEARNED THROUGH LOVE AND AFFECTION

Years ago, after a newborn was brought home from the hospital, mommy and baby were both placed on what used to be referred to as the three-month rule. The three-month rule suggested that neither mommy nor baby leaves the house until the baby was at least three months old, unless of course there was an emergency, they were going to the doctor's office, or the mother had to go back to work. Many mothers were open to this idea because they loved having that time to bond with their babies and appreciated being able to rest as their bodies healed. In support of this tradition, it was a standard practice for family members, neighbors, and friends to run errands and do as much as they could to be of help. Of course, there were still some parents that had to be coerced into understanding that having a baby was ultimately the beginning of the "It's not all about you" phase. Years ago, there were people, namely the older women in the community, who were more than happy to expand on that entire speech to anyone who didn't understand it. Today, some people are just not being taught to take their newborn baby's health into consideration before deciding whether or not they will take the baby out in public—the mall, the grocery store, nail or hair salons—just because they can, as though the baby is an accessory. Some women even feel that because they have sacrificed their bodies for up to ten months carrying their child, they should not have to be "stuck" inside the house after the baby had been born. In the past, there were mothers, grandmothers, aunts, and sisters who would step in to help take care of an infant in the event that the mother did not or could not, for whatever reason, take time out to do so. Today, those support systems are slowly fading away. Three months was once considered a reasonable amount of time for a baby's immune system to begin the building process, for a mother's body to begin the healing process, and a nice amount of time set aside for a mother and a child to bond.

Through this, we learned what it meant to sacrifice our time for the benefit of someone else.

PATIENCE LEARNED THROUGH NURTURING A BABY AT HOME

"Do not have that baby outside in the nighttime air" was a common phrase heard years ago. It was not popular in the past as it is today to have children outside during the nighttime hours. For some reason, still unknown to me, it seemed that many of us became sick or came down with sore throats after being outside at night for long periods of time. Although some people felt that this theory was just an old wives' tale, many of us still seemed to be affected. Because my mother didn't like having us out at night running errands, when she had something to do that she wasn't able to fit within the week's schedule, we were forced to get up with her early on Saturday mornings, and take care of those things then. I can remember being a young girl and my mother, like a bus driver, waking us up around 7:00 a.m. for us to go everywhere we needed to go for the day. We must have made it to the grocery store, shopping mall, car repair shop, and—on a special day—the movies, and still seemed to be home by 2:00 p.m. As kids, we were really looking forward to sleeping in late and lying up in bed watching cartoons until the last one went off. And don't get me wrong, there were definitely days that we watched our fair share of Saturday-morning cartoons; but if there were places to go, we were up and at them and back home before the day was done. I couldn't appreciate the process then because I didn't really understand it, but as an adult looking back on it, I'm happy that I wasn't out in the street at all times and was allowed to live within the structure of a child. When parents had things to do in the evening that couldn't be rescheduled, they'd ask a family friend or relative to come and sit with their children while they were out. It's funny how creative they were even in figuring out ways that would allow them to have fun with their friends but still keep their children's well-being a priority. Many parents decided to host dinner parties at their homes instead of going out in the town, which made it easier on them as well as their friends who had children because the host's children did not have to leave the house and their guests' children were bundled up and were only out for a short period of time.

We learned to utilize the daytime hours as much as possible, but when we had to be out, we always stayed bundled up.

PATIENCE LEARNED THROUGH AVOIDING NIGHTTIME AIR

I can remember hearing my mother say, "Sometimes, you may have to fight for your child in order to help them develop into the person that you know that they can be." Over time, I realized that this meant that parents have to be willing to go the distance and sometimes almost be in a fight with their child, about their child, in order to help them to make the right decisions. Our parents chose to settle certain battles with us early on in our lives, and although it took a lot of patience for them to not give up and push us to the point of understanding, they did it because they understood what they were fighting for. Back then, a child's punishment was often made to be a clear reflection of whatever they had done wrong or a miniature version of the punishment that they would have received had they done the same thing as an adult. It was normally something that was memorable enough for them to never want to do it again. For example, a child who stole money from someone was forced to work odd jobs to earn enough money to pay that person back, and those who set fires were sometimes taken to visit burn victims so that they could see the direct result of their actions. In the past a lot of people did their own home improvements and if kid threw a baseball into someone's window and broke it, they were made to give up their Saturday activities and help to install a new window. These old-school lessons helped to draw a straight line for us from our problem to a solution, which made us better understand our situation. We were shown through example that it is better for a parent to be firm and to punish their own children out of love than to have a police officer or judge punish them with no regard for their well-being. Fighting for a child to make it out into the world as a decent adult rather than giving up and saying that it is just too hard requires that parents exercise a lot of patience, especially when dealing with children who were like us and were considered to be headstrong or hardheaded. My mother said that because GOD had never given up on her, she decided to never give up on her children.

Over time, we learned to appreciate the fact that our parents weren't fighting with us but fighting for us. It gave us a better understanding as we became parents that wanting to be a nurturer but needing to be a disciplinarian can be exhausting and that the "fight for your child" moments are those that help us to remember that it is a job to be a parent.

PATIENCE LEARNED THROUGH GOING THE DISTANCE WITH AND FOR YOUR CHILD

The anticipation that came with hearing our parents say the words "Wait until I get home" when speaking to us over the phone after we had done something wrong seemed to create more of a panic than the thought of the punishment itself. We would sit at home in a state of complete nervousness, not knowing what was going to happen when they arrived. "Wait until I get home" was usually followed by the instructions to turn the TV and/or radio off, not to get on the phone with friends, and not to go outside and play. We were basically forced to be patient and actually sit there and wait until our parents got there to let us know how we were going to be punished. We were too afraid to leave, and many of us had learned through our past experiences that it was best not to completely disrespect our parents and disobey them any further. We also knew that if our parents asked our neighbors if they had seen us outside, they would tell everything that they knew. It only took one time for me to hear my mom ask some one as she walked up to the house, "Has BeNeca been outside this afternoon?" and him saying, "Oh yeah, I saw her out there talking to her friends until right before you arrived." That caused insult to injury but taught me how to sit still and face my consequences.

Through this, we learned to be responsible for our actions and accept the consequences that followed.

PATIENCE LEARNED THROUGH WAITING UNTIL OUR PARENTS GOT HOME

Some of the most important lessons were taught to us through the simplest exercises. For example, we learned a lot about building patience by sitting outside on the porch in an old T-shirt with a pomegranate. My mom would buy the fruit for us and let us sit out there, eat, and enjoy ourselves for however long it took us to finish it. Because each seed inside of a pomegranate is covered with pulp, we learned how to enjoy taking the time to eat from each seed. After sitting outside for hours trying to finish all of it, we always walked away feeling as though we had been given a lot of something special to enjoy. It was something very simple that kept us busy, out of our mom's hair, and excited about having a treat. What sticks out most about this memory is the patience that we developed from taking the time to eat from one seed at a time. Parents seemed to be more creative in their approach to teach their children certain lessons years ago. Although as a society we may have less time in our schedule, it is still important that we teach our children how and what it means to have patience and that everything good does not come from immediate gratification. The funny thing is that I just recently found out that many people eat the pulp with the seed. Thanks to my mother, I had no idea that the seed was even edible. I laughed so loud when I found out because I realized how clever she was. After we were taught how to create something beautiful from a diamond that was still in its rough stage, we were more willing to not only look for a diamond but to also appreciate the fun in scrubbing, buffing, and shining it as well. Many children today are not expected to be patient and are given a diamond on a chain or in a ring with no lesson, no conversation, and no sense of appreciated value attached. Status symbols are supposed to be symbols of one's individual status. When a child has worked for nothing but starts with his or her status at a level of luxury, his or her perception of the time that it may take to build something from the beginning stages is often distorted.

From this, we learned that although some goals take a longer amount of time to achieve and may appear to be challenging, by tackling one piece at a time, we can still accomplish our goals.

PATIENCE LEARNED THROUGH EATING A POMEGRANATE

One value that was sewn into the stitching of our character at a very early age had to do with our responsibility to help others.

We learned that it was our duty to not only look and listen out for ourselves and our family but to also look out for the people who lived around us. We were expected to be of assistance to our neighbors as much as possible. "Being neighborly" was a phrase commonly used that was synonymous with being kind, friendly, and helpful to our neighbors and something that we were encouraged to do on a regular basis through firsthand experience. It was a bit like mandatory community service. Whenever one of our neighbors was sick, our mother would send us to their home with soup, medicine, and any other remedy that she saw fit to help them in their time of need. Although we didn't have an official neighborhood watch program or welcoming committee, it was understood that all the neighbors in the neighborhood were watching out for each other on a regular basis. Most people paid close attention to those who moved in to the neighborhood. Some walked freshly baked desserts over to a new neighbors' home as they welcomed them in to the community and found out more about them. Back then it was common for people to have everyday conversations with their neighbors and even borrow things like cups of sugar and flour from one another when they were in need to help tie them over until they were able to go to the store for themselves. This system was so effective because people understood that favors could always be reciprocated. Nowadays, borrowing sugar from a neighbor is not only unheard of but also considered by many to be intrusive. Some people are comfortable with having others live near them as long as they don't have to lend them anything or speak to them when they don't feel like it. A question like "How are you doing?" that was once only asked when someone genuinely wanted to know how you were doing so that if there was anything that you needed, they could help you, has lost much of its sincerity. Today it is used as a greeting in the same manner as saying hello. There was a time when people communicated with each other in an attempt to build genuine relationships. Now, many only establish relationships when they think that there is some benefit in it for them. As kids, we were made to deliver whatever was needed to the hungry, sick, and elderly. In the beginning, we definitely complained about how mean some of the seniors were to us or that some of their houses smelled funny, and we begged our parents not to make us go back.

Over time though, through this community service, we learned more about the lives of people that we helped and grew to have compassion for them. Eventually many began to open up and talk to us about their circumstances. We learned that older people were just younger people at heart whose bodies had began to age and that they often used grouchiness as a defense when they thought that they were about to be judged by someone who didn't understand their situation. We learned that when someone said, "I don't need your help," what he or she really meant was "I don't want to have to be in this situation where I need your help. I would like to be able to do this on my own like I used to be able to." We found out that the smells in their homes were a combination of the food they were forced to eat due to their health conditions as well as all the medications and creams that they needed to use in order to make themselves feel better. They shared stories about their hard financial times, children who never came by to visit, and family members whom they had outlived and really missed. As we began to listen to their stories, we learned to appreciate them more and realized that they were like walking history books. They were able to share all that they had experienced through their many decades of life. Because we live in different times, our children have been made to be more cautious than we were when getting to know new people. However, if we teach them to have a spirit of kindness and a willingness to give, they will have an open heart to help the people that they know.

This tradition taught us to have a spirit of kindness and to be helpful to others. It also helped us to understand how our community service serviced our community.

PATIENCE LEARNED THROUGH BEING "NEIGHBORLY" AND HELPING OTHERS

"I'm bored" was once a forbidden phrase for children to use at one point in time. It was like saying a bad word if your parent was in the room because everybody would stop talking and wait on their reaction. Being bored means being tired of and slightly annoyed by a situation that is not interesting, exciting, or entertaining. It was okay for us to be tired from doing our chores or schoolwork, but to complain that we were bored was like asking our parents to add time onto their schedule to "entertain us." They felt that if they had to entertain us, it would unnecessarily be adding more work for them to have to do, especially considering that they had already provided us with things like paper, pens, crayons, and other tools that we could have used in conjunction with our imagination to make ourselves happy. For those of us who had sisters and brothers to play with or talk to, there was no excuse accepted. Because our parents worked so hard during their lives within their careers and helped to take care of their entire family, they seldom had the opportunity to be bored. They thought that we only felt this way because we had either not taken the time to use our imagination and think of something that we could do for ourselves or we had too much time to relax. If it was viewed that we were complaining about having too much time to relax, they would ask questions like "You're bored? Did you clean your room, the kitchen, sweep the floor, etc.?" If, by chance, we had actually done those things, we would then be told to go outside and sit on the porch or play. After hearing that speech a few times, we learned to just go outside and sit on the porch and play when we started to get bored, which taught us to use our imagination and kept us from having to go back into the house where our parents were guaranteed to find something for us to do. With televisions, video games, and DVD players that can be taken almost anywhere, there is no wonder why children today feel that they are bored when they are not being hand-fed their every thought. We have a tendency to give children more information than we allow them to think about on their own. Why should they sit, be quite, and listen to their surroundings when they could so easily be entertained by something else? Some of our short-term solutions have long-term side effects. For instance, some children who are constantly entertained by DVD players in the car act out of control when the DVD player is denied. Are we unconsciously raising children to not know how to be creative and use their imaginations? Although there are positive electronic devices that focus on education, it is very important that they are taught to be well-rounded and how to use several different educational methods as a way of learning. Children who develop long attention spans not only benefits in their classroom but also on their job and in their personal lives.

Through this lesson, we learned how to have an attention span that lasted longer than a few minutes and how to entertain ourselves.

PATIENCE LEARNED THROUGH COMPLAINING ABOUT BEING BORED

As toddlers, with the exception of when we were in our own home where we knew all the house rules and safety precautions, we were always expected to be where someone could see us. Our parents didn't want us to run into anything that we didn't know would be there and could cause us harm. For that reason, when we went outside to play, if whoever was taking care of us didn't come outside with us, we were required to always stay where someone could see us. We could play on the porch or in the yard as long as we stayed within their eyesight. Of course we wanted to go out of the yard with the older kids but had to learn how to be patient and wait until we were old enough and our parents said it was okay for us to join them. In this day and age, when toddlers are being kidnapped from outside of their own front gate, it's very important that parents keep an eye out on their children.

This reminded us that our parents cared about our safety and were always looking out for us.

PATIENCE LEARNED THROUGH STAYING WHERE OUR PARENTS COULD SEE US

Once we were no longer toddlers, we were allowed to leave our front yard and play on the block with the rest of the kids. However, there was a common rule that applied to all the younger children in the neighborhood. It was the "four houses down" rule that stated that we were not allowed to play, skate, or ride our bikes or big wheels farther than four houses down the street in either direction from our house. We didn't complain about it or find it to be a hard rule to follow because we were just so happy that we were finally old enough to go beyond the front yard and did not have to sit with the toddlers anymore. We were looking forward to the new adventures and remembered how slow things seemed to be in the front yard in comparison to the newfound sidewalk outside of our gate. We considered it to be a big deal and realized that the alternative would only take us one step backward. With all the older kids already out in the neighborhood, it made us feel that we were one step closer to being like them. When children have something to compare their situation to, it builds their appreciation for their current situation.

We learned to appreciate the little things in our lives as though they were the biggest things in the world by remembering that as we push forward, we could always fall backward.

PATIENCE LEARNED THROUGH PLAYING NO FARTHER THAN FOUR HOUSES DOWN THE STREET

The neighborhood curfew that was reserved for the older kids was set by the streetlights that were scheduled to come on as soon as it started to get dark outside. When the streetlights came on, we were expected to be on our way into the house or we were in trouble. Being "on our way into the house" did not mean running down the street, walking through the gate, or talking on the porch to our friends. It actually meant standing in the doorway with at least one foot in the house. Asking to stay out longer than curfew was not something that we begged to do often because that request earned us a mouthful of a lecture filled with questions about why we thought it was even necessary for us to stay outside at night. Older people used to use the phrase "Trouble lurks in the dark," and because safety was definitely a concern, we were not given the opportunity to be outside at that time. Our parents didn't want to have to worry about being outside looking for us out in the dark if something happened. Although if someone didn't come home, it was a normal sight to see their parents walking down the street looking for them, and it was no fun at all when they were found. It was a complete embarrassment. Other kids who saw someone's mom walking down the street would say to each other from their windows things like "Look! Jimmy's mom is walking down the street looking for him." They'd laugh because most times they knew where he was and what was going to happen when he got caught. This taught us, as teenagers, to be where we were supposed to be at the time we were supposed to be there. If we didn't obey this rule, we would be held accountable and would not be able to go outside at all for some time. The streetlights added a bit of safety to the streets for the children who were still on their way home for whatever reason. It is unfortunate that some cities have found it acceptable to give more weight to conserving the city's budget than to safety.

This was another building block toward being responsible and accountable in our lives.

PATIENCE LEARNED THROUGH COMING HOME BEFORE THE STREETLIGHTS CAME ON

As children, we walked to as many places as our parents would allow us to. Walking to school, a friend's house, or a store were just a few of our common stomping grounds. We didn't complain about having to walk because we considered it to be a step toward our independence. It was something that we could do with our friends that became a social event as well as a great form of exercise that helped us to burn off some of our energy. The reality of it was that even though we felt as though we *got* to walk, we had to walk. Unlike today, our parents did not burn their gasoline driving us to the corner store when we were more than capable of walking. As we became teenagers, after successfully mastering walking around the neighborhood and being responsible enough to come right back home, we were then introduced to and taught how to use the public transportation system in our area. Depending on the location, kids learned how to ride the bus, train, BART (Bay Area Rapid Transit) trolley, subway, or whatever type of public transportation was nearby. This was a way that our parents helped us to become even more independent and responsible. Being allowed to travel across town to the mall or movies using the public transportation system was a sign to others as well as to ourselves that we were maturing and becoming trustworthy. As kids we felt that only the "big kids" were allowed to do things like that, and if our parents trusted us that much, we felt that we must have been moving in the right direction. We were required to know not only how to get from one location to another and back home by the time the streetlights came on, but also how to properly budget the money that we were given that was to last us for the day. Between paying for our transportation to and from wherever we were going and possibly splitting the rest between food and fun forced us to plan and use the money management skills that we had been taught. If we lost or mismanaged our funds and had to ask our parents to come and pick us up, we knew that our privileges of "being on our own" would be taken away until they felt that we could handle them. Once we were old enough to learn how to drive, we already knew how to walk and take the public transportation systems everywhere that we needed to go, which helped to balance our viewpoint on how much of a privilege being able to drive actually was. Driving required a certain level of maturity, wisdom, and respect for other people's property, namely our parents' car. It was also understood that while we were driving our parents' car, their rules still applied. Once we learned how to drive, we learned that "to whom much is given, much is required." This meant that with our new driving privileges, we were expected to do things like run errands for our household and quickly found out that our mom no longer had to be the only person responsible for things like grocery shopping. We were also required to pick up our siblings from school as well as any other family member who might have needed a ride, without complaint. And believe me, within a lot of families, there always seemed to be at least one aunt or uncle who needed a ride to and from the doctor's office and felt that the new kid with the license really had nothing better to do than to tote around everyone who had some place to go. We didn't complain much out loud however about the extra responsibilities because we were just so happy that someone trusted us to drive.

We were guided to take baby steps in life in order to appreciate each level that we were given the opportunity to stand on. Taking the small steps built the confidence that we needed to continue to climb toward another. Climbing steps one by one helped us to feel and appreciate the foundation under our feet.

PATIENCE LEARNED THROUGH TAKING BABY STEPS (WALKING, RIDING, AND DRIVING)

Remember when school shopping was an event? Well, maybe you don't. However, for so many of us, it was the one time of the year that we knew (hoped and prayed) that we were going to get new clothes. There was a method and somewhat of a ritual about the process because our school clothes were expected to last us throughout the entire school year. Our parents usually bought enough for us to be able to wear new clothes for the first week of school, and then they expected us to incorporate our old clothes with the new. This was a very exciting time. Kids today do not seem to know much about the school-shopping rituals of yesterday because many parents buy so many clothes throughout the whole year just because something is "cute." Years ago, families set priorities on their budget, and clothes were not high on the list. If our parents could provide us with a house to live in and still manage to pay the household bills and put food on the table and clothes on our backs, they were satisfied. Clothes didn't get thrown away or tossed to the side as quickly as they do now. Just because there was a hole in the knee of our pants did not mean that we needed or were getting a new pair. The hole was easily fixed by covering it with a patch of fabric. Eventually, once we realized that we were not getting a new pair of pants no matter how we felt about it, we learned to change our perception, embrace our situation, and let our patch stand out. We found that true "style" bloomed out of some of the most interesting circumstances. Now, many years later, designer patches are sold in stores to be put on to pants that do not even have holes in them. Today, a lot of children are being taught to value the wrong things, and priorities are not always being set properly. We were not happy about not getting everything we asked for, but later in life we were able to say "Although it bothered me sometimes that I didn't have all the new clothes that some of the other kids had, once I was able to understand what my parents were able to accomplish by saving their money, I realized that I can have anything but just cannot have everything."

We learned to appreciate what our parents were able to provide for us as well as the example that they set.

PATIENCE LEARNED THROUGH THE RULES OF SCHOOL SHOPPING

Putting things on layaway was once a common method used to buy things from department stores. It was a very common way people bought school clothes for their children. Our parents started buying our school clothes for the new school year during the summertime. They'd take us to the department store and let us try on the clothes that we liked to see how they fit. Because they were being purchased so early, we were still expected to grow before the school year started; and since they needed to last us for the entire school year, we always bought our clothes in a size slightly larger than what we wore at the time that we tried them on so that they could be adjusted to fit us properly as we grew. After it was decided what we were going to buy, our parents would have the store manager lay them away in a storage room for a small fee until our parents were able to pay off the total amount due. They would make payments every time they got paid until the bill was paid in full. Instead of complaining that we didn't get to take the clothes home at the moment that we picked them out, we got so excited because we knew that we were going to get new clothes. In a society where trends change so quickly, some people are afraid to lay clothes away, fearing that they won't be in style once they are able to pick them up and take them home. My mother always said that we should look for well-tailored clothes at a bargain because cheap clothes go out of style, but well-tailored clothes can last a lifetime. The layaway process helped us to understand that money didn't just appear out of thin air but that our parents worked hard every day to provide for us. Because we went with them to make the payments, we saw firsthand how they divided their paycheck between the many aspects of life. We realized that buying our clothes was just one part of our family's budget.

This process taught us to have patience and to appreciate and take care of the things that were given to us. We learned what it felt like to truly look forward to receiving something.

PATIENCE LEARNED THROUGH PUTTING CLOTHES ON LAYAWAY

What is now considered to be normal involvement within parent-pre-teenage relationships at school has changed over the years in some places. When we became preteens, our perception of our school grounds changed as we started to view it as our own world. It was our own place. With the exception of back-to-school nights, parent-teacher conferences, or special events, our parents weren't seen hanging around very often. Of course, they still let us know that they were paying attention to what we were doing, who our friends were, and even asked a lot of questions about what we did at school; but they just didn't get overly involved for different reasons. Some people didn't have the time to spend their days at their children's school due to their work schedules, while others felt as though middle school was the time that their child needed to be given the opportunity to feel as though they were able to live a little in what they had been taught. My mom felt confident that she had already taken the time to teach us how to exercise proper behavior. We knew that we were to obey the school rules, do our work, and get good grades. It was pretty simple. Although my parents were capable of helping me with my homework, they were quick to say "That's not my homework" or ask "Weren't you paying attention in class?" This was not intended to be harsh, but it reminded us that we were to be responsible for our own work. It helped us to be more independent and to realize that sometimes in life we would only have ourselves to depend on. The extra space that we were given at school helped us to widen our perception of our own reality and be more aware that we were a part of a society at an early age, it helped us to be more comfortable as we entered into what we consider to be the real world. Dealing with everyday workloads, social issues, and activities and making decisions about people and problems at school became very helpful as we went through those same issues as adults. Because we were able to start making more decisions on our own in middle school our confidence in our own judgment grew tremendously. As we began to make the right decisions and became more independent, we were then encouraged to continue to walk in the right direction.

This was a lesson that made us realize that we would not always be able to depend on our parents and, in many situations, would need to pay more attention to the things that pertained to our individual lives.

PATIENCE LEARNED THROUGH ALLOWING A CHILD TO BECOME MORE INDEPENDENT DURING THEIR MIDDLE SCHOOL YEARS

One of our household rules, once we were in middle school, stated that if our homework was finished and our chores were done, we were then allowed to talk on the phone with our friends. We were each given a fifteen-minute time limit on the phone. This did not mean that we could talk to each one of our friends for fifteen minutes at a time but instead meant that we had fifteen minutes of total talk time to be on the phone. My mom understood the importance of allowing us to practice and develop our social skills. Although she wanted us to be able to socialize with our friends, she did not see why it was necessary for us to sit and talk on the phone for long periods of time and felt that after the first fifteen minutes or so, most children are either looking for something to talk about or are talking about other people. This rule helped to prevent us from becoming little chatterboxes who were so used to talking that we never stopped. Unlike today when many young kids have their own private phone lines in their rooms so that they can have private time to have private phone calls that their parents aren't privy to, our phone line was not private at all. We had been warned that we should always watch what we say because we may never know who might be listening. We knew that our parents could pick up the phone at any time to use it themselves and overhear our conversation. Overtime, that in itself helped us to realize that if we couldn't say certain things with our parents listening, we probably shouldn't say them at all. Eventually my mom got tired of sharing the phone with us and had another line installed that was strictly for her use. However, this didn't mean that the old family line then became our own personal phone with special privileges held just for us because the same rules still applied. Although she didn't pick up the phone to listen in to our conversations, I don't think, we knew that she could if she wanted to.

This helped us to understand that talking on the phone was for the purpose of exchanging information and not just for sitting by the phone wasting time. It helped us to better understand time limits and to respect the time of those who might be waiting in line.

PATIENCE LEARNED THROUGH HAVING A FIFTEEN-MINUTE LIMIT ON THE TELEPHONE

Most people did not own cell phones when I was growing up, and those who did didn't allow their children to use them on a daily basis. There were no "But, Mom, I really need a new cell phone so that you can reach me if you need to" conversations. Although we lived in the city and walked to and from school, we knew that it was a part of our responsibility to call our parents and check in with them as soon as we walked through the door of wherever it was that we were going. Some parents who couldn't receive personal calls while they were at work set up a system where their kids had to call their job and let the phone ring a certain number of times to signal to their parent that they had made it in safely, and the parents would then call them later when they were on their break to see how they were doing. For those who had jobs where phone calls were not possible at all, children were required to check in with and be accountable to some other adult. Our parents' mind-set was different than many of today. When my daughter was in the sixth grade she came home one day and said, "Mom, if you buy me a cell phone, you will never have to worry about where I am because you can just call me, and I'll tell you." And I said to her like the parents of yesterday, "If you are where we discussed that you would be, I won't have to look for you because I'll know where you are." She, just as I did, had to gain a clear understanding that kids are supposed to be where they were told to be, with no exception, unless they received permission to do something different. Times have definitely changed, and our society is more dangerous than ever before. Providing a cell phone for a child when they are out of their parents' sight can definitely put minds at ease, but a lot of these children practically never leave their parents' sight except when they are at school but still proclaim to need a phone. For some kids, cell phones can be a distraction that take time away from the time that they could be doing something more constructive than having a casual conversation. Many can no longer appreciate the conversations that people are having right in front of them because they have developed a reaction to always be ready to get on the phone or text their friends to hear about the next conversation and what somebody else has to say. The fact that there are now no cell phone policies in some elementary schools is mind-boggling. We have to direct our children to focus on the more important things in life. Every moment spent takes time from another. It is important for children to learn how to prioritize their time, but it is also important that we as parents help guide them to make good decisions. We must ask ourselves if what we are allowing our children to choose to do is important enough to use up their time or if we allow it because it prevents them from using up ours.

We learned to have the patience to appreciate and enjoy the time spent with the people who were right in front of us rather than continuously looking for the next best conversation to be had with someone else.

PATIENCE LEARNED THROUGH WAITING TO HAVE CELL PHONE PRIVILEGES

My mom was happy to provide us with the things that we asked for but always wanted to know all the details involved in the request. When we would say things like "Mom, I need twenty dollars for my field trip," she would immediately ask, "Where are you going? What will it be used for, and when do you need it?" Of course, just like most kids, we really wanted her to give us the money sooner than later so that we could hold on to it and have it in our pockets just for the sake of having it in our pockets. She would however always give it to us on the day that it was due. She didn't want us to lose it before we needed it and wanted us to learn how to wait patiently for the things that we ask for. We knew better than to get on her nerves and bug her about it because that would only lead her to being irritated and ultimately telling us that we would never get it if we were not patient. If we had a field trip and the money was due on the tenth, we received it on the tenth. I remember hearing people say to kids, "I have enough to worry about, and you are not going to worry me about this." This process helped us later in life to realize that worrying about something before the deadline is due is a waste of energy. We often agonize over things that we need weeks, often months, before they are actually required. As an adult, I sometimes remind myself to get back into this mind-set, and it helps me to put things into perspective and lessens my stress. As children, if we had already asked for money for one thing and then needed additional money for something else, we had to ask for the additional money in a separate conversation. We weren't given the opportunity to say "I need more money because I spent the first twenty dollars you have given me on something else, and now I need more." We learned that although our parents may have wanted to do everything for us that we asked them to do, oftentimes they needed to take each request and look at it in comparison to where they were with their budget, and then plan accordingly. Understanding this taught us not only to be very specific about the things that we wanted but also to prioritize the things that we asked for according to what we knew or felt was most important to us.

We learned to ask and plan ahead for the things that we wanted. This taught us to trust our parents when they said that we would have something when we needed it and not to worry unnecessarily, but understand that as long as we have what we need when it is required, we are okay.

PATIENCE LEARNED THROUGH WAITING TO RECEIVE SOMETHING UNTIL IT IS ACTUALLY NEEDED

CHAPTER THREE

Hold My Hand

Hold My Hand

This chapter reminds us of methods that were once used to teach children about the importance of having guidance and discipline in their lives. Being that all children are not the same, using different methods may be necessary when working with them based on their individual personalities and circumstances. However, all methods generally drive down the same road of understanding and appreciating structure and consequences.

GUIDANCE TAUGHT THROUGH:

A parent's unconditional love

Holding someone's hand

Home training

Structure and discipline

Naps and bedtimes

Teaching responsibility beyond today

Having immediate consequences

The official "Grocery Store" Rule

Learning about appreciation

Preventative healthcare

Minding our manners

The support of our village

Parent-Teacher relationships

Eating right, exercising and playtime

Being held accountable

Being cautious

The rituals of school clothes, play clothes and dress clothes

The "Open Door" policy

Preventing the unnecessary

Turning our heads

Having parents who stayed "Plugged In"

Writing reality checks

Time management

Consideration

Setting boundaries

THREE

Growing up, I remember hearing people say, "No one will ever love you like your parents." As a child, I didn't completely understand what that phrase meant in its entirety. I thought that it meant that once someone was given the job of being a parent, they were supplied with a certain type of love that only they could give to their child. As I got older, I realized that this phrase was actually referring to the fact that in most cases, no one in your life will love and guide you as unconditionally as your parents will. No one will provide for all your needs and finance your life's invoices while teaching you how to do so for yourself, neither will most people deal with all your problems while making sure that every aspect of your life is okay. We, like many kids, often thought during the times when we were in trouble that our lives would be so much easier if we lived at someone else's house. I can remember my mother telling me that although someone else may have made sure that I had fun and felt comfortable while I was at their home, no one would take care of all of the things that she took care of for me on a day-to-day basis. She reminded me that those people could afford to take care of some of my wants because she had already taken care of my needs. Some children grow up thinking that everything that their parents have done for them is customary and that everyone they meet should try just as hard to make sure that they are taken care of in the same way their parents have. It is essential for children to understand that a parent's love, guidance, and structure are intentionally elevated to the highest level out of the love that they have for their children. Of course, there are exceptions; but in many cases, no one will love a child like their parents.

Understanding our parents' love helped us to build a level of appreciation for them as well as a realistic point of view of what other people were not required to do for us.

GUIDANCE THROUGH A PARENT'S UNCONDITIONAL LOVE

As early as the days when we learned how to walk, our family started guiding us all along our way. We were taught to hold their hands and follow their direction while walking alongside their every move. Wherever we were going, be it down the street or through a crowded store, as children we learned to look for someone's hand for guidance. Of course, there were times when we wanted to walk ahead by ourselves and felt that we no longer needed to hold anyone's hand, but we soon found out that their guidance was still necessary. I remember being in a department store with my mom one day and sliding my hand out of hers as I tried to walk ahead on my own. She decided to watch me as I tested the waters. When I finally realized that she was no longer beside me, I went into a panic in my own little world and I started getting nervous. After a minute or so, she stepped out from where she was standing and just stood there, held her hand out, and said, "Now the next time I tell you to hold my hand, hold my hand." Times like these taught me that sometimes I might need more guidance or direction than I think. Even as siblings, we were instructed to make sure that if we were not holding on to our parents' hands, we were holding on to each other. Through this, we learned the importance of being accountable for one another as well as making sure that everyone around us was okay. The older kids who were guiding the younger kids learned to pay attention as they moved forward with the understanding that someone else was following their footsteps.

Through this we learned how to follow direction, recognize the guidance that was given to us, and that we were to always look out for each other.

GUIDANCE THROUGH HOLDING SOMEONE'S HAND

The phrase "home training" once referred to all the lessons that parents took the time to teach their children while they were at home that then gave a proper perspective on how to behave whenever they were somewhere else. Our parents made it very clear to us what they considered to be "proper behavior," which usually depended on where we were and the circumstances that we were faced with. During the times when we found ourselves somewhere that we were unfamiliar with what the proper etiquette was supposed to be, we were expected to "act" as though we knew what to do, even if it just meant standing still, being quiet and polite. Years ago, parents were very sensitive about having to be stressed out because one of their children was acting out of control and misbehaving. Of course, as children we all tried to get away with certain things but, for the most part, tried any "new behaviors" at home first so that we could find out what our parents' reaction would be. Even children who got into trouble quite a bit usually knew better than to try any new challenging acts in public without first having a proper testing at home. It's funny because even today, when a child is acting up in public, it is still common to hear an older person say "You can tell that that child has had no home training." This simply means that judging from the child's behavior, it's obvious that his or her parents did not take the time while they were at home to teach the child how to behave outside. When people say that they cannot "take their children out in public without the children acting out of control and causing a scene," it seems that what they are really saying is that they have not made the time or that it's not worth the effort and headache to teach their children how to behave. Some people feel that it is sometimes just easier to leave them at home in hopes that the child is going through a phase that they will eventually grow out of, that someone else will teach their child how to behave, or that the child will teach themselves what's best.

We learned how to behave properly while we were at home.

GUIDANCE THROUGH HOME TRAINING

Growing up, we became very familiar with the words *structure* and *discipline*. They were blended into the cement that was laid on the foundation of our lives, which ultimately held all our values together. They were very significant in our house because my mother felt that it was important that we had a solid base to build our lives on. The structured patterns that she laid down for us when we were kids taught us how to create structure in our own lives as we became teenagers and adults. It also provided us with a sense of stability and made us feel safe. We equated having structure with having someone who cared enough about us to make sure that we were being taken care of every day in the exact same way. We also learned that when our parents made us do something over and over, it was not because we were being punished for doing it wrong the first time, but because they wanted to make sure we knew how to do it right from that point on. My mom would say things to me like "This lesson is not for my benefit because I already know how to do what I am sitting here *trying* to teach you." She also reminded me that I would eventually move out of her house and be on my own and would need to know and understand certain things about life. The effort that was put forth to discipline us as children taught us how to discipline ourselves as adults. We learned how to make decisions based on what we had been taught, our past experiences, and what we thought would be the best decisions for our future. Our parents loved us so much that they took time out of their life's schedule to teach us the difference between what was right and what was wrong. Some today feel as though they are doing their children a favor by not providing them with structure and discipline but instead letting them find their own way. Interestingly enough, over time, we associated structure with security and discipline with caring.

Although we didn't always appreciate the structural walls that were built for us or like going through the motions of being disciplined, eventually we learned that they were both set in place for our benefit out of love.

GUIDANCE TAUGHT THROUGH STRUCTURE AND DISCIPLINE

Years ago, taking a nap or going to sleep for a short period of time was viewed as something that every child needed to do at some point every day. I can remember having to take naps until I was about nine or ten years old. As children, it helped to adjust our attitudes when we were tired even though we used to do everything we could to get out of having to go lie down. It wasn't something we loved to do, and we usually felt that if we fell asleep, we would be missing something. However, because our parents knew what was best for us as a whole they made sure that we took our afternoon naps. Today, many only refer to taking naps as a form of punishment for children. I find that theory to be interesting because children get tired from their day's activities in the same way that adults do. However, unlike adults, many children do not know how to express the fact that they are tired and are in desperate need of taking a break. Because of that, their attitudes sometimes begin to change for the worst. Along with the disappearance of naps, bedtimes seem to be slowly becoming obsolete in many households as well. *Bedtime* was a regular vocabulary word in our household. We had a set time to go to sleep until we were about sixteen or seventeen years old and were completely able to regulate our own schedule. Once we were given the opportunity to stay up a little later, we then had to prove that we could handle the responsibility that came with it. We had to make sure that we did not miss a beat. Today some kids are allowed to fall asleep whenever they please, are staying up until late hours of the night on a regular basis, and have learned how to just get by on a few hours of sleep. This can cause a lack of focus in their classrooms and, in some cases, lead teachers to test and enroll students into less-challenging classes when in fact, they may just be sleep deprived on a regular basis. Taking a nap and going to bed by a certain time was not an optional feature on the kiddie menu when I was little but a mandatory perk. Bedtimes not only benefit children but also their parents. It allows parents to have a little time to unwind and even have uninterrupted conversations with other adults before getting into bed. Having a bedtime routine and taking scheduled naps added structure to our day. Although it may be hard to get children into a routine, once they are in it, their bodies will usually, naturally adjust to their schedule. Children who take a nap at the same time every day generally get sleepy at the same time every day. Structure is one thing that a lot of kids fight and yet crave at the same time. Some are having tantrums when they're sleepy and are looking for someone to hold them and tell them that it is okay for them to go to sleep. As adults, we too sometimes need someone to tell us that it's okay for us to just stop and rest. Understanding how we are affected by this should encourage us to incorporate naps into the lives of our children so that they too can be as productive as they are able to be in their own lives.

As we got older, we realized that taking naps and getting enough sleep helped us to live more productive lives.

GUIDANCE TAUGHT THROUGH NAPS AND BEDTIME

On several occasions, I can remember my mother saying, when speaking to us about the things that she made a conscious effort to instill in us, "If I should die today, there are certain things about life that I need to make sure that you are aware of and know how to do." Because of her views on this matter, she made sure that there were certain basic things that I absolutely knew how to do. For instance, I understood at an early age that I was to always pay close attention to street names and cross streets whenever I was traveling so that in case of an emergency, I would know how to get back to wherever I was taken from. I also knew how to do things like write a check, operate an ATM, and cook and clean up after myself by the time I was eight or nine years old. Because in the past many of us were trained how to do so many things at such a young age, some people vowed that they would never make their children do those same things but would allow them to have more freedom and less responsibility than we did. However, over time, it became apparent that many of the lessons that we learned made us more responsible and helped to build our character. Our parents felt that it was crucial for them to talk to us about all the little, yet important things that they wanted to make sure that we understood. This made me become aware of the fact that some people do not have the opportunity to see their children through every phase of their lives, and because of this, I decided to share whatever lessons cross my mind during the day with my kids while I have the opportunity to do so. I realized that raising my children beyond my every day with them is very important. It's necessary as a parent to understand that if something tragic should happen to you, most people are not going to raise your child in the exact same manner that you would have. They would have no way of knowing all the little pieces of random information that you would have shared with your child.

We learned to put certain lessons in our "pockets of life" so that regardless of what might happen in our future, we would have those things to pull out when we needed them.

GUIDANCE THROUGH TEACHING RESPONSIBILITY BEYOND TODAY

Our parents were quick to "meet us where we were" so to speak as it pertained to the consequences of our actions. When we were bold enough to do something that we knew we were not supposed to do, our parents were bold enough to discipline us right where we were no matter who was around. When I was about twelve years old, my friend decided that she was going to sneak out of her house and go to a neighborhood party even though she had been specifically told that she could not go. As soon as her mother realized that she had left the house anyway, her mother got into her car, drove down the street to the party, knocked on the door, found my friend, and then told her to go home right away. Instead of giving her a ride back to their house and saving her daughter from being completely embarrassed in front of her friends, she told her to walk home the same way that she had walked to the party, as she then drove slowly alongside her daughter saying, "Oh, I see that you do what you want to do. I got your number." For quite some time, the neighborhood kids teased my friend by saying, "Your mom's got your number." Nevertheless, after this happened, she always thought twice about doing something like that again because she remembered the consequences that she faced before. Our parents were quick to remind us that if we did not want to be embarrassed outside in front of our friends, we should not do things that would cause us any embarrassment. This not only made us consider our actions but also taught us to think twice about how we would feel if we were caught in the act. Children often need to instantly make the connection between something that they did wrong and the punishment that they receive. In some cases, when parents wait too late to acknowledge that they are aware of what their child has done, the child assumes that he or she have gotten away with what he or she did and does it again before the parents have taken the time to address the issue.

Being punished right after we had been caught doing something wrong had a longer, lasting effect on our decision not to make the same mistake again.

GUIDANCE TAUGHT THROUGH HAVING IMMEDIATE CONSEQUENCES

Before the days when people completely ignored children who lay out on the floor of grocery stores while having extreme tantrums when they did not get their way, there was what was known to many of us as the official grocery store rule. This rule was said to us right before we walked in the store as a friendly reminder of why we came in the first place so that we would keep our minds focused on our purpose. The full version was said something like "Now when we get into this store, do not look for anything, do not ask for anything, and do not touch anything. We are only going in here for—amount of things and nothing else, so please do not ask." If we decided to stray away from or forget what we had been told, rather than our parents repeating themselves to us, they would look at us and quietly say, "Now what did I tell you before we came into this store?" We all tried at least a few times as little kids to get around it by begging for something that was not on our list but learned that unless our parents offered to buy us something extra, it was best to keep to the plan. We learned that no matter what we saw other children do, we had to go home with our parents who did not play the tantrum game.

Self-control, self-denial, and focus were the lessons learned from this rule. We learned to control ourselves in the store and refrain from pleading for things that we were not going to get. This helped us, as adults, to realize that we do not need to buy everything that we see just because we might have enough money to do so. It also taught us that when we are shopping, we should always make a list of the items that are needed and avoid buying things that are unnecessary.

GUIDANCE TAUGHT THROUGH THE OFFICAL "GROCERY STORE" RULE

As children, we were not given the most but taught to appreciate the least. So often, I hear parents who are upset complain that their children do not appreciate all the things that they have given them. Most children, after being given one toy, will typically make an attempt to explore all the possibilities in which it can be used before their interests die. However, when they become accustomed to being given several toys at once, they will not always take the time to explore all of the possibilities because they are constantly looking to see what may be given to them next. When I was younger, Christmas stockings were traditionally filled with inexpensive little trinkets that were viewed as "just a little something extra." Most families that could afford to give them away filled them with things like candies, fruits, and nuts and the fancier stockings included things like small toys. Although this tradition has continued, today's stockings are being filled with things like iPods, MP3 players, and PS2s. When those are the least expensive gifts given, what message are we sending to our children? When my children were toddlers, I would allow them to open all their Christmas gifts on Christmas Day to make sure they knew what they had received and from whom the gifts were from. They were then allowed to choose three toys that they wanted to play with immediately, and the rest were put into their closet until they had completely worn-out their initial selections. I found that this process helped them to truly be grateful for each toy. They were encouraged to take their time with each one, looking at it and studying every possibility. They did not complain about only getting three because they were excited about the three that had been given to them. Even now when their appreciation levels run low and I notice that they are not truly appreciating something that they have, they are given less in an effort to help them appreciate more. Somehow, this practice seems to adjust their levels quickly. If children are never made to climb the stairs in life, they will never fully appreciate life's elevator rides.

We learned to appreciate whatever we were given.

GUIDANCE THROUGH LEARNING ABOUT APPRECIATION

What happened to the days when babies were always dressed in undershirts, socks, hats, jackets, and blankets that were draped over them whenever it was cold outside? During the wintertime when we were growing up, we were not allowed to go outside without wearing our jackets, hats, and gloves. Even on average days, we were required to wear undershirts and socks with every outfit as a method used to remind us of how important it is to take care of our health. It is upsetting for me to see little ones outside dressed in almost nothing during the cold season, especially when their parents are dressed according to the weather. Not having all of today's cold medicines, advanced technology, and health insurance plans, our parents understood the need to enforce preventative health care. Getting sick in those days was viewed as a serious and potentially deadly problem. Today, society seems to be less concerned about what could happen but instead rely more on the hopes of being able to treat health problems when they occur. Before sports shoes endorsed by basketball players and other celebrities became popular for infants to wear, people made a point of buying walking shoes that gave great support to their child's feet as they learned to walk properly. Although walking shoes still exist today, they are not as popular as they used to be because of all of the newer, trendier styles that are out there to choose from. This is a great example of how having too many options can sometimes make it harder for one to make the right decisions. We may have only owned a few pairs of shoes as children, but they were always sturdy, of good quality, and well-structured. Our parents shopped at Stride Rite and Buster Brown for our shoes until they could no longer find our sizes. I remember when my daughter was about three months old and someone had given her the cutest pair of shoes. I was so excited that I ran to show them to my mother. The first thing that she said after picking them up was "Those are really cute, but I know you are not going to put those heavy shoes on her little feet. She will not be able to lift her legs up while wearing them." My mom's statement reminded me, as a new mother that my baby's health was more important than how she looked like in her outfit.

These small lessons taught us about preventative health care, which helped us to create habits that became beneficial to us during our lives. Walking shoes taught us a lesson at a very early age about taking care of our entire body. We might not have liked the way that our shoes looked, but we were taught that they were used as a tool to help our feet develop properly.

GUIDANCE THROUGH PREVENTATIVE HEALTH CARE

"Mind your manners" was something that was said to us whenever we were doing something that was considered rude, as a reminder of the manners that we were supposed to be using at that time. There were once things that were thought to be high on the list of having good manners, and asking to be excused in certain circumstances was one of them. The phrase "Excuse me" was used as a key that allowed us to enter into and exit out of certain situations. We had to ask to be excused whenever we walked into a room where there were people already present, in case we were interrupting something that they were doing before we walked in. By doing this, we were acknowledging that we were aware that they were there before we got there and that we were not coming into their space as though we discovered it. This kept us from growing up with a sense of entitlement or assuming that whenever we entered a room, everyone there was supposed to run up to us as we arrived. It taught us that whenever we come to a new place, we should say hello, introduce ourselves, and find our way in someone else's space until it becomes our own. Asking to be excused was also mandatory whenever we were interrupting other people's conversation, as our way of recognizing that we understood that what we needed to say may not have been any more important than the conversation that they were already having. It was also expected that we would ask to be excused whenever we were passing by someone in close quarters, as a polite way of asking that they excuse us for brushing up against or coming so close to them. Because coming together and sharing a meal as a family was a common tradition that required everyone's attendance, being excused and having to leave the dinner table earlier than the other people at the table was another situation where giving an excuse was expected. Something else that was considered to be rude was showing up to a dinner or party empty-handed. We were taught that if we're invited to an event, we should always ask the host if there is something that we should bring. Of course, our family and friends welcomed us whether or not we were able to bring anything with us, but this taught us the importance of contributing to whatever we were involved in.

Minding our manners helped us to get in the habit of being polite, put us in the mind-set to always add to whatever we are given which helped us to see the importance of contributing to our community and society. The lack of manners in today's children is only acceptable because we have decided to accept it as normal.

GUIDANCE THROUGH MINDING OUR MANNERS

The structural walls of a community were once built by the support of the people who lived there. This is what made the old saying "It takes a village to raise a child" so relevant. There was a time when it was instinctive for everyone to look and listen out for any child who was nearby no matter whose child it was. People generally felt a strong sense of responsibility to help each other and to always make sure that children were always taken care of. Whether there was a need for food, clothes, or discipline, anyone in the neighborhood who saw the need filled it. People did not wait to get permission to be of help; it was just something that they did because they saw it as the right thing to do. If one of the mothers in the neighborhood sensed that a child was hungry, she would offer to feed him or her, and because people knew how to make food stretch, they were always willing to share whatever they had and feed any child in need. Unfortunately, because of the society that we now live in, we can no longer trust that it is safe to eat from everyone's kitchen. Back then, if a child walked past wearing clothes that did not fit them properly, people made an effort to help in whatever way they could. The clothes that they gave to them might not have been brand-new but were "new to me" clothes, which were also known as hand-me-downs. Hand-me-downs were once very well received by all. Of course, we all loved new clothes but got excited about our "new to me" clothes as well. There was a whole system to it. For example; mothers who knew of a child in the neighborhood who was in need of clothes and wore a size or two smaller than her own child would generally donate her child's entire wardrobe to that child on a regular basis once her child outgrew them. People who didn't know of a specific child in need usually boxed up their children's clothes once they no longer fit and stored them away until they either found someone whom they could give them to or donated them to their church or local Salvation Army. Having too much pride, "keeping up with the Joneses," and the playing the brand-name game put donating clothes to other people's children out of business. Offering constructive discipline to a child in need was also something that was once well received and free of charge. In the past, anyone who saw a child do something wrong would say something to them first, and then immediately tell the child's parents not only what happened but also what their personal response was to the situation. Today, many parents suffer from the "No one is allowed to talk to my child" syndrome. Some even argue with anyone who makes an attempt to talk to their child in an effort to merely teach them a lesson that, quite frankly, they should have taken the time to teach them in the first place. What's even worse is when parents actually see their child do something wrong, choose not to say anything, but still yells at the adult who tried to help their child. As children, one of the things that kept us focused when we thought about doing something wrong when our parents were not around was the fact that we knew that there were other people who were watching what we were doing and had no problem speaking up and telling our parents about anything that they witnessed. Adults at one point in time took control of their neighborhoods and were not concerned with or afraid of what the children thought about it. Our neighbors showed how much they cared about us by taking time out of their lives to get involved in ours. The conversations and actions that were taken to support us as children within our community, served as the bricks of the walls that were built to protect us.

We learned that it is important to stay involved and support the needs of our neighbors as well as our entire neighborhood.

GUIDANCE THROUGH THE SUPPORT OF OUR VILLAGE

"**D**on't make me leave my job early" was once a common phrase used to remind us to stay out of trouble when we were at school and our parents were at work. Back then, there were a lot of people who did not really like their jobs and only went to work to provide for their family. Having to ask their employer to leave work early to deal with their child's disciplinary issues not only jeopardized their family's financial security but also embarrassed them. They felt that it was like making a public announcement that although they were trying very hard to be good parents, they were failing. When we were little and got into trouble at school, our teachers and administrators served as a part of our "village." They were quick to talk to us about our actions and were trained to deal with problems as soon as they happened. They took a sense of responsibility with each child who crossed their path. After they spoke with a child who had gotten into trouble, in extreme cases, the child's parent would be called to come to the school to join in the conversation and add to the resolution. There were no secret parent conferences held between parents and teachers as there are in some schools today because it was understood that a child should be aware that their parents and teachers were in constant communication about how they were doing in school. Once the parents arrived, everything was discussed out in the open between the parent, teacher, and child. Because there was a connection between our parents and teachers, we knew that there was not much that we would be able to get away with at school that our parents would not instantly find out about. Although I always loved going to school, participating in class, and being involved in the activities, homework was never my thing. I can remember being in the third grade and "forgetting" to do my homework one too many times. My teacher explained to me why I was in trouble, called my mother, and told me that I was going to have to sit in her class in detention until someone came to pick me up. She cared enough about me to spend her personal time that she was not getting paid for to stay with me in an effort to teach me a lesson. For that, I will always appreciate her. My daughter once asked me, "Mommy, why is it that every year on the first day of school you always tell my teacher your name, phone number, and e-mail address when it's already on all our paperwork in the office?" I explained to her that it is because I like to be the first to know about a problem or misunderstanding the moment that it happens so that we can fix it before it gets out of hand. In the past, after the parent conferences were over, parents were provided with a private area that allowed them to talk to their child to determine an appropriate punishment or solution to the problem. Today, it seems that school staff members are being trained not to be *hands-on* but to only *observe and report* the actions of the students as well as the parents. Many parents these days are made to feel as though in troubled times, the staff members are only there to act as therapists or social workers to approve or disapprove of the methods of discipline chosen rather than act as a part of the process. It's hard to complain about a child's behavior if parents are not allowed to parent their child. At the same time, it's hard for teachers to partner with parents who do not want anyone saying anything to their child from a disciplinary standpoint. When children are sent to school, their behaviors are not left at home. Therefore, we as parents must be open and be appreciative of the observations given by those who are asked to help with our children on a daily basis. With class sizes as large as they are today, I found that it is necessary for me to make sure that I have a personal connection with my children's teachers.

We learned that our parents and teacher communicated about the things that were going on in our lives, which encouraged us to behave properly.

GUIDANCE THROUGH PARENT-TEACHER RELATIONSHIPS

We hear so much in the media these days about how many children have stopped playing outside and that today's youth are struggling from obesity at higher rates than ever before. Some say it is because of all the junk food that they are eating on a daily basis; but honestly, we ate more than our fair share of candies, chips, cookies, and cakes. Things were different for us however because most of our breakfasts, lunches, and dinners were pretty healthy meals. Even the kids who ate food in the school cafeteria were encouraged to eat their vegetables and fruits. We ate foods like real (not instant) oatmeal, Cream of Wheat, and toast and eggs and pancakes and sausage for breakfast. Our lunches included sandwiches, fruit, milk, and juice on a daily basis; and dinners were made from fresh, not over processed greens, peas, and other vegetables that added nourishment to our bodies and helped to balance our diets. Of course, we were always excited to go to fast food restaurants because we didn't get to go every day but were taken as an every-now-and-then special treat. The fact that we didn't always have the money to eat out all the time really helped us maintain a healthier lifestyle. Another thing that helped us stay fit was the fact that we had the benefit of attending schools that had mandatory physical education programs that were held every day. There are schools today whose PE classes only meet two to three times a week at best. Somewhere along the line, someone thought that exercise as it relates to a child's health was low on the list of priorities, and because of this, the program has fallen short in many schools. We not only exercised at school but then also came home and played outside for hours on end with other neighborhood kids. Those of us who were a little nervous or shy and didn't want to go outside and play with the other children were encouraged to go introduce ourselves because our parents knew that we would more than likely make new friends and appreciate the process in the long run. Parents loved the fact that children exercised and played outside because it helped them to stay in shape, release any pent-up energy, and sleep better. When children have no "village" to depend on, there's no one there to encourage them to eat right or watch out for them as they play outside.

From this, we learned the importance of incorporating healthy foods with fun snacks, playing outside, and socializing with other people.

GUIDANCE THROUGH EATING RIGHT, EXERCISING AND PLAYTIME

Oftentimes, our parents would send us to the neighborhood store with a list of items to buy. On occasion, we would be allowed to use a portion of their change to buy something for ourselves, which was always very exciting because it made us feel as though we had our own money to spend, and were able to make our own choices based on the amount of money that we were given. I remember walking through the store, spending a lot of time browsing, looking at this and looking at that, while trying to figure out whether or not I had enough money to pay for all the things that I wanted. The experience itself was just as much fun as having the things that I bought. My mom would occasionally remind me that although sometimes she let me take a little bit of her change for myself, I should never expect that the change would be given to me. She'd sometimes say, "Make sure you bring me back my change" and would make mention if there was even a quarter missing from what she knew was due back to her. This was not something that she pointed out because she needed the quarter but because she wanted me to know what it felt like to be held accountable. She also wanted me to know that I was not entitled to keep things that belonged to other people that had not been given to me.

This was our initial lesson on how to budget our finances properly. Having to add the prices of potential items that we wanted at the store before we got them to the counter in an effort to make sure that we had enough money to buy them taught us to count quickly. We also learned the importance of counting the change that was given back to us and making sure that it was correct, checking the receipt to make sure that we were charged the correct amounts, and returning the change to whoever gave us the money in the first place.

GUIDANCE THROUGH BEING HELD ACCOUNTABLE

"Trouble lurks in the dark" was a common phrase used to warn and remind us that there were certain places that we should not be once it was dark outside and that it was always best for us to stay where we could be seen and protected. Because trouble did not only "lurk in the dark," there was a list of other places that we were not allowed to be without supervision or for what our parents considered to be "for no good reason." Although we were encouraged to play outside with our friends, we were not allowed to hang out in their homes unnecessarily, and the thought of spending the night as small children was absolutely out of the question. We weren't socially deprived and had sleepovers, but they were typically with our cousins and/or other family members. If my mother knew our friends' parents, we had a better chance of being able to go over to their houses to visit with them. But, oftentimes, that could have just been the reason that we were not allowed to play inside of their homes. My mom would say that it takes only one time for something to happen that could change our lives forever. Today, people often label that type of concerned parent as being overprotective. She was not overprotective but was just not willing to put us at risk over something that she did not see as necessary. One of her duties as a mother was to think about the unforeseen in an attempt to protect us. She took her stance with that position and did not waiver from it. Looking back on it, I realized that this did not rob us of our social experience because we were after all allowed to play with our friends all day at school and after school. Her viewpoints taught us to be cautious about our surroundings and the choices that we made in life. We live in a time when things have definitely changed. The fact that communities were at one time smaller and families knew more about each other made it easier for us as children to play with other children because our families were more familiar with not only their family but also their household. With communities continuously getting bigger, we should be more encouraged to take the time to get to know the home environment of families we allow our children to visit with. It is essential to know if there are other siblings or family members that live in the house and, if so, to know more information about them. Spending time at the home of my child's friend in order to feel out the vibe is vital. If I feel out of place about asking to stay for a little while when dropping my child off, I need to ask myself, "Why do I feel uncomfortable about being here, getting to know this child's family, but feel comfortable enough to leave my child here alone with them? Am I allowing my child to be in an environment based only on his or her own intuition?"

We learned to pay attention to safety within our environment.

GUIDANCE THROUGH BEING CAUTIOUS

When I was growing up, we had three categories of clothes: school clothes, play clothes, and dress clothes. Because we were expected to take care of our school clothes so that they would last for our entire school year, part of our daily routine after coming home from school was taking them off and then getting dressed into what we called our play clothes before we went outside to play. Even though our school clothes may not have been the most expensive, we were still expected to take good care of them and my mom would have a fit if she drove up and saw us playing outside in them. This practice taught us to understand that if we take care of our things, they will last longer. Our play clothes were either old clothes that were good enough to play outside in but not decent enough to wear to school or were handed down to us by someone else and had already been worn quite a few times. Because many mothers were excellent seamstresses, we never seemed to throw old clothes away that were still in good condition because they could be transformed into something else that we could get good use of. Pants that we grew out of and became too short were then cut and stitched along the bottoms and made into a nice pair of shorts. Pants that were not fit to patch up or make shorts out of but decent enough to wear outside became our play clothes. Shoes that were scuffed up too badly to wear to school but still fit became shoes that we played in. This helped us to see the value in being able to get the most out of everything. Some of the clothes that we played in were even purchased from thrift or secondhand stores. Although they may have only cost fifty cents a piece, we were happy because after all they were "new to me" clothes that allowed us to play outside freely. Back then, kids lived to go outside and play, so anything that helped the process was considered to be great. And besides, it was not optional. We had to go outside and play. Today's kids have been given the option of whether or not they would like to play outside. Many would rather be inside playing video games, chatting on the computer or just choosing not to get their brand-name outfits dirty. We enjoyed being outside in our play clothes because that was our free time to run and play with our friends without having to worry about getting in trouble for getting dirty or playing too rough. We were able to be kids to the fullest. It seemed fun to have different clothes for different times. We wore our *dress* or *fancy* clothes on Sundays, holidays, and special occasions, and it was a pretty big deal that we looked forward to. Little girls didn't just put on dresses but oftentimes also put on petticoats, stockings or tights, gloves, fancy hats, dress shoes, sweaters, and whatever else added a little extra to their outfits. Little boys were often seen wearing dress shirts, ties, dress socks, and jackets. In homes where there wasn't an abundance of money, it was still important that the children felt good about how they looked and were still given, in many cases, the opportunity to get dressed up as well. Given that a lot of families made their own clothes, it was not uncommon to see siblings dressed nicely in outfits that were all made out of the same fabric. Because it was thought by some that families who came from lower financial backgrounds weren't expected to look decent or respectable in the eyes of society, many parents made an extra effort to make sure that their children looked nice and neat when they went outside. Getting dressed up in a new dress from the store or my mother's sewing machine was very exciting and always a fun time.

Having school clothes and shoes taught us that there was a time and place for everything and to take care of and appreciate all things that were given to us. It also helped us to understand the concept of getting dressed appropriately for work or wherever we may need to go. Although people today are often ridiculed when they get the most use out of some things before throwing them away, the concept of having play clothes taught us the value in utilizing everything to the fullest. Because we were taught to take pride in our appearance, when we got dressed up, we really got dressed up. This taught us that regardless of whether or not we have the same amount of money as the person standing next to us, we are to always make the best out of what we have and walk with the same level of confidence as everyone else.

GUIDANCE THROUGH THE RITUALS OF SCHOOL CLOTHES, PLAY CLOTHES, AND DRESS CLOTHES

As small children, we operated under what was known to us as the open-door policy. This policy stated that our bedroom doors were to be typically left open. Our parents never had to worry about what we were doing while we were in our bedrooms by ourselves because at any given moment they would walk by and take the time to see what we were doing. Of course, we received the privacy that we needed to get dressed; but other than that, as little children, the doors were usually kept open. I do not think our parents ever thought twice about what effect that might have had on us. It was more important to them to stay connected to what we were doing than to focus on a rule about a child's privacy. As teenagers, things were different and we were given a lot more space to roam around. However, it was understood that our parents still had the right to knock on our door and check in to see what we were up to. We gained a very clear understanding that our bedroom door really belonged to our parents and the fact that we were able to say it was "our" door was something that they allowed us to say to make us feel more comfortable in our environment. At some point in modern times, many children have been given the impression that their bedrooms are *literally* their rooms and that they can do anything that they want in it. Stores started selling signs in pretty pinks and blues that read "Stay out!" and parents started buying them, saying that they were cute. Children started slamming doors in their parents' faces saying things like "This is my room!" If we ever had anything smart-mouthed to say about "our door," we were given the speech about how we didn't own any doors in the house, and it was a privilege for us to be able to say that we had a room (even if we were sharing it); and if we decided to get too radical about our viewpoints, we just might find the door in the garage with a sign hanging from it stating that we have no say-so about the house rules.

This little rule reminded us that no secrets were to be kept from our parents in their house. We learned to do everything in the light instead of the dark, which kept us in the habit of being honest. It also made us appreciate having a room that we were allowed to call our own.

GUIDANCE THROUGH THE "OPEN-DOOR" POLICY

Having friends of the opposite sex in our bedrooms was not even thought of as a question that was okay to be asked. We grew up during an era when a character by the name of Smokey the Bear, who was known for helping to prevent forest fires, was very popular. My mother was like Smokey the Bear when it came to us playing with boys inside our house. She felt that because most children are curious by nature, it was easier to prevent certain "fires" from happening than to deal with the consequences after the fact. Once I was allowed to date, my boyfriends were welcomed to come over to sit and visit but were restricted to staying in the living room, kitchen, and other open areas. There was never a reason good enough for my mom to allow them to hang out in my bedroom. Many people during that time felt that allowing boys and girls to hang out in their bedrooms together with no supervision was like putting a match in a fire and hoping that it will not burn. We were kept out of harm's way as much as possible because many of us had adults around us who were interested in preserving our childhood and innocence for as long as possible. We were educated on subject matters that dealt with sexuality and talked to about how our body, emotions, and hormones all worked together. However, we were introduced to those topics in the bits and pieces that our minds could digest and were not put into certain positions and then expected to make adult-like decisions.

We learned how not to put ourselves in certain situations as a preventative method of staying safe.

GUIDANCE THROUGH PREVENTING THE UNNECESSARY

There was once a time when people looked forward to coming home and watching their favorite television shows with their families. It was a big deal because they couldn't wait to find out what their favorite characters were going to say next and how the plot was going to thicken. Most of today's programming however seems to be based around how realistic the violent scenes can be or who is dating who; and because the shows that go over the top with these subjects generally have higher ratings, the regard for what children are exposed to even on daytime television has become secondary. When I was younger there were certainly some things that we were not allowed to watch, but they were not as over the top as they are today. For one, shows that were considered risqué didn't come on until after 10:00 p.m. and we were in the bed by then. And two, our parents would always tell us to "turn our heads" whenever we were watching a television show or a movie and a scene came on that showed something that was considered to be inappropriate for us to watch. If something that was violent, scary, or involved people lying in bed together a little too close for our eyes to see, we were instructed to turn our heads until we were given permission to turn back around. Because many of the cartoons on the air today are filled with adult content, parents are either finding themselves restricting their children from watching an entire show or are just giving up and allowing their children to watch these shows, feeling like there is nothing that they can do about it. Because many television shows that were once considered late-night programming now start at 8:00 p.m., bedtimes in many households are not being enforced, some parents refuse to miss their favorite show in spite of the fact that their child is in the room, and there are those who will not tell their child to "turn his or her head" we now have a generation of young children who have seen too much and talk about things that they have no real understanding of. I remember being in my early twenties or so and hearing a group of young parents who were defending their reasons for allowing their children to watch certain shows. They were saying that it wasn't a big deal because their children would eventually see those images anyway. Growing up in a family day care environment, I saw children mimicking things that they had been exposed to but had no real understanding of. Children go from seeing to doing a lot faster when they are introduced to things firsthand. Now that the television has become a babysitter and programs do not seem to sell without the minimum amounts of sex, bad language, violence, and adult humor, it is no wonder why some children speak the way that they do about certain things. When children attack other children, be it a violent crime or rapes, people always ask "Where did they get that from?" Many children imitate things that they have witnessed even though they often don't understand why.

Having to "turn our heads" away from the things that were not age appropriate for us to see helped to preserve our innocence and taught us that there were certain things that we were not quite ready to see or understand.

GUIDANCE THROUGH TURNING OUR HEADS

Although there wasn't a concern about children meeting pedophiles on the Internet years ago because the Internet was not used in the same manner as it is today, had things been the same, this probably would not have been as much of an issue because our parents paid so much attention to what we were doing all the time. Our lives were filled with constant questions: "So, what are you up to?" "What do you have going on today?" "Who was that on the phone?" and "Who is going to be there?" Video games were the biggest deal and closest thing in technology that we had to the Internet, and we owned quite a few games. My mom made sure that they met her standards, and she knew firsthand that none of them encouraged us to steal cars, had secret chat rooms, sexual subtleties, violence beyond repair, or anything to that effect. She took the time to play many of them with us and sat and watched us play the others so that she was aware of what was being planted into our minds. She was just as active in approving the music that we were allowed to listen to. I will never forget the day when my mother took a hot needle and literally burned the lyrics right off an album that was bought for us. She didn't have a problem with the entire album, but there was something on the end that was not okay for us to hear at that time, so she decided to take it right off. I had never seen anyone else do that before and thought it was just the craziest thing, but looking back on it now, I can appreciate it. Because we live during a time when people are singing about "licking lollipops," "sipping syrup," and subtly suggesting that when it gets too hot outside, we should all want to take off all our clothes, when my children were toddlers, I would always tell them that they could not sing the lyrics to songs that they did not fully understand or felt uncomfortable explaining. This kept them from talking about things that they knew nothing about and made them more conscious about whatever they decided to say. Checking in with children to see what they are doing while on their computer or out with their friends, what they are listening to on the radio, what the video games that they are playing are about, and every other area of their lives keeps parents plugged in to their children. There is a big difference between being intrusive and being informed. People often say when finding out something devastating about their child's action that they had no idea about anything that was going on.

We learned that our parents stayed plugged in to our lives in an effort to keep us safe.

GUIDANCE THROUGH HAVING PARENTS WHO STAYED PLUGGED IN

There have probably always been children who ran away from their homes for serious reasons or even to go off to get married and jump-start their lives without getting their parents' permission. Many of us, after getting into trouble, thought about how much better we thought our lives would be if we no longer lived with our parents. We daydreamed about how much they would miss us and the devastation that would occur if we were to leave. Some of us went as far as to try to threaten our parents by saying that we were going to run away because we didn't think we were being treated fairly. We quickly learned that those words meant nothing to them and that we were not threatening their lives but putting our own lives in jeopardy. Parents were big on writing reality checks or giving us a clear picture of our reality when our mind-set seemed to be a little distorted. My mother, just like many other mothers who were told their children would be running away, then pulled out the "run away" speech and said, "Go right ahead. Let's see how far you get out there. And do not bother calling any of your aunts, uncles, cousins, or grandparents because I talked to them before you were born and let them know that if you ever tried anything like this, they were not to let you in but to send you right back home to me. I can't believe that you would want to leave this house where I pay all the bills and try to teach you about life. So . . . when you do not want to follow my rules, you think it's just that easy to run away? Well, let's just see." As children we generally had one of two reactions. Either we were so worn-out after hearing that speech and just went to our room or were told to go on outside and were left out there on the porch until we begged to come back into the very house that we threatened to run away from. It is comical how imaginative our parents were at showing us how to put our troubles into perspective and showing us our reality. Nowadays, many people are more concerned about their children's reaction to being disciplined than they are about the lesson that they should be teaching them through the discipline itself. These days if someone saw a child sitting on a porch crying as they learned their lesson, they might be quick to call the police and report what they had seen as some sort of abuse rather than just finding out if the child was okay. When people only report what they see but don't want to get involved even in the least bit, it leaves them trying to add a solution to a word problem that they have not yet read and know nothing about. However, for us "third generation country" parents, we have no problem explaining the lesson being taught to our child if and when a officer arrives. Certain lessons have a bigger impact and bring an immediate reality to little children while the world still seems too big to them. Someone once told me that his fifth-grade class went on a field trip to their local town jail. Although it seemed extreme to me at first, he explained that because he was so little, the jail seemed so big which made the impact everlasting. He vowed at that time that he never wanted to go back under any circumstance.

We learned that extreme behaviors can bring extreme consequences.

GUIDANCE THROUGH WRITING REALITY CHECKS

The words "Be where you are supposed to be when you are supposed to be there" as they related to someone picking us up and giving us a ride somewhere that we needed to go were very important to understand. It was the beginning of our lessons on properly managing our time for not only ourselves but to also meet other people's deadlines. Our parents had no intention of running around our school or the shopping mall looking for us. It was considered to be disrespectful for us to expect that the person who came to give us a ride should have to find us first. When we were younger, if my mother had to look for us, we were in big trouble. However, once we were teenagers, if we left her waiting for an extended period of time, we found ourselves having to either wait for her to get back home so that we could call her and ask if she would come right back, trying to negotiate a ride with someone else's parents who were on their way, or catching the bus home. Through the trial and errors of our experiences and being told to "Be ready where you're supposed to be, and don't have me waiting when I come to pick you up," we learned to respect other people's time and appreciate their kindness. Many parents trained their children early on about this and understood that either their children were on their schedule or they were on the children's schedule. This lesson was not about having patience with a child but a matter of teaching a child to have respect for other people's time. When people do not learn this early on in life, they spend their lives asking others to wait on them or are often left behind.

Through this lesson, we learned to respect other people's time and to understand that if someone came to pick us up, it meant that they took time out of their schedule to help us, even though they could have been doing something else.

GUIDANCE THROUGH TIME MANAGEMENT

My mother didn't mind taking my friends home from school, the mall, or wherever we were coming from, but she became upset if I waited until she came to pick me up and was in front of my friends to ask if it would be okay in hopes that she wouldn't say no in front of them. She didn't like feeling as if I was manipulating the situation to work in my favor. The time when I waited until she arrived to ask her, she took my friend home, but once we were alone, I got lectured about taking her for granted. She said, "Do not wait until I am there to pick you up to ask me to take your friends home!" and then explained that sometimes after a hard day at work, she did not feel good, was tired, or had made other plans for the night that did not include my friends. We learned that it was not okay to assume that our priorities would be someone else's and that other people have nothing more important to do than what we request.

Through this, we learned how to be considerate and that we should never take people for granted or assume that they have nothing better to do with their time other than what we need them to do.

It also taught us to plan ahead, ask for the things that we want in advance, and that we should not put other people in positions that make them feel uncomfortable.

GUIDANCE THROUGH CONSIDERATION

Whether it was one of our friends or someone who we were dating, at a certain time in the evening, our friends had to go home. Even though we were at home, unless someone was spending the night at our house, there was still a curfew set for how late our friends were allowed to hang out there. I can remember my mom calling us into her room many a time and saying, "It's time for your friend to go home." That was our cue to pack up the visit and say good night. Although we didn't appreciate or fully understand the logic behind this growing up, eventually it taught us to prioritize our time and that at some point people should allow us to have our own personal space. As kids, my friends were not allowed to just sit around our home and hang out all night. Now as an adult, although I can appreciate having company come over and visit, I can also appreciate my personal quiet time at home.

Through this, I learned that there is a time and place for everything and setting boundaries in my life helps other people respect my personal space. It also taught me how to let people know with a smile, confidence, and without feeling guilty when I am ready to have a little time to myself.

GUIDANCE THROUGH SETTING BOUNDARIES

CHAPTER FOUR

Home Sweet Home

Home Sweet Home

We received such great training about so many aspects of life just by being at home. This chapter breaks down many of the lessons learned that we were able to incorporate into our daily lives.

HOME TRAINED IN:

Respecting our parent's home

Exercising good judgment

Never responding to a blowing horn

Making quick decisions

Conserving everything

Respecting other people's property

Saving money

Planting and picking our own seeds of health

Cooking from scratch

Utilizing staples

Making something out of nothing

Appreciating our meals

Understanding that our kitchen was not a twenty-four-hour diner

Understanding that there were no "Save-Me-Somes"

The Value of Cleanliness

FOUR

Our parents had a ready-made speech that they used to remind us to whom the house we lived in really belonged to whenever we started to act as though we had forgotten. They would say "This is my house. After you have gone to school, graduated, and gotten yourself a good job, you will then be able to have a house too. That is the house where you will be able to make up all the rules, but until then, you will abide by my house rules." This reminded us that we did not manage or have any control over anything, except for ourselves, that happened in their house where we lived. The funny thing about it is that this phrase pushed us to graduate from school so that we could find a job and get our own house where we could make up all the rules.

We learned that different people have different rules for how they like their home to function. This helped us later on in our lives to respect and adapt a lot easier to the space that belonged to other people. We also learned that whoever pays for something generally has the most control over what happens with it.

HOME TRAINED IN RESPECTING OUR PARENTS' HOME

My mom didn't allow a lot of people to run in and out of our house on a regular basis, and we were definitely not allowed to have company over when she was not home. She would say "Don't have your friends running through my house when I am not here." However, she usually had no problem with our friends coming over when she or another adult was there. My sister and

I used to have a friend who lived in our neighborhood who we played with all the time. One day while my mom was at work, or so we thought, our friend called to find out what we were doing and if she could come over. After we told her that we were cleaning up and she offered to help us, we looked at the clock and decided that it was a good idea to let her come over. What we didn't know was that my mom was well on her way home. Just as our friend was washing the dishes, I was cleaning the counter, and my sister was cleaning the living room, we all—seemingly at the same time—heard keys jingling at the front door. My friend then dropped the plate that she was holding as we all just froze in place. Needless to say, we were on punishment for quite some time for disregarding her house rule and having our friend over even though she was not home. My mother was so mad and disappointed in us. Seeing what her reaction was about having one friend over without her permission kept us from ever even thinking about having house parties without the proper consent. We learned to respect her home.

We learned to exercise good judgment based on the lessons that we had already been taught.

HOME TRAINED IN EXERCISING GOOD JUDGEMENT

One thing that was thought of as being extremely rude and many could not stand for people to do as they drove up to their homes was to blow their horn as they arrived. When someone came to pick me up and they blew their horn instead of getting out of the car, my mom would get so upset and start asking all kinds of questions like, "what kind of person would be so impatient that they would blow their horn and assume that someone would just run outside as soon as they heard the sound?" People in those days were expected to get out of their car, knock on the door, introduce themselves, and state and/or reconfirm the plans for the outing. I can remember a time or two when I was a teenager hearing a horn blowing outside and my mom saying, "You'd better not run out there. Wait for them to get out of the car and come to the door." It didn't really matter who was picking us up because the rule applied to everybody. We realized how serious she was about the subject after my friend's mother pulled up to our house one day to pick me up and practically laid her body on her car's horn to let me know that she was ready for me to come out. My mom went outside and shared her views on the subject. We learned from that point on to forewarn people and ask them to please get out of the car when they arrived. I would always tell my friends "Do not blow the horn when you drive up to my house because if you do, I will not be allowed to go." My mom didn't want me hanging out with people she felt didn't have enough home training to get out of their car and knock on the door. It was only really uncomfortable when my friends were too young to drive and I had to have them ask their mothers not to blow their horn. Some didn't understand at first, but eventually, everyone grew to respect her wishes.

We learned that blowing the horn was often a reflection of how people expected us to respond to their demands and that we should not get used to running to everyone's beck and call general in life.

HOME TRAINED IN NEVER RESPONDING TO A BLOWING HORN

There was no such thing as running in and out the house when we were outside playing. We were often told, "If you come in the house one more time, you're in for the day." That option seemed to be more like a punishment because being outside made us feel free but once we went inside, we were confined to the many chores that always needed to be done. But there was just something about running back and forth that we couldn't resist. It seemed to add a lot of fun and excitement to whatever we were doing until we were caught. We used so many excuses on why we needed to run back and forth like "I have to go to the bathroom," "I forgot something," "I have to put something up," or "I am thirsty." Whatever our excuse, after a few times of running in and out, we had to make a decision on where we wanted to be, inside or outside. The doors opening and closing seemed to cause quite a few problems. Between the flies that flew into the house, the cool air being let in or out depending on the season, and the older people's nerves that just could not take the slamming doors and constant movement, it was said to be a pretty big deal.

This rule taught us about setting priorities and decision making at an early age.

HOME TRAINED IN MAKING QUICK DECISIONS

Turning the lights off as we exited a room, even when we were coming right back, was a mandatory, standard practice. Even though we did not know as much as we do today about wasting energy, we knew a lot about wasting money and were forced to conserve on everything. There was no wasting water. If we didn't have a full load of clothes and only had one item of clothing that needed to be washed, we were forced to hand wash and air-dry that item or wait until someone else was planning on washing their clothes and add it to their load. I remember having to go around the house and ask everyone if they had any white clothes so that I could add their clothes to what I needed to wash in order to make a full load. Leaving the refrigerator door open for long periods of time also seemed to cause an upset. We were reminded that by doing so, we were not only wasting electricity but also burning out the light bulb faster than necessary. We learned how to conserve in an effort to make things last longer. Today there are many campaigns asking people to conserve in the same areas that our mothers and grandmothers forced upon us as we were growing up. Learning to save anything for whatever reason be it financial or environmental is helpful and is better for the world as a whole.

We learned the values in conservation.

HOME TRAINED IN CONSERVING EVERYTHING

As little kids, we were always on a scavenger hunt for interesting things to find. We played and looked for things outside as well as all over the house. However, there was one room that we knew we were not to be caught playing in, and that room belonged to our parents. We were certainly always welcomed to come in to their room with their permission to watch television with them or lay in their bed when we were sick, but we understood that we could not just wander into their room because we felt like it. Because every other part of the house had already been given to us to roam around in, their bedroom became the only place of peace and personal space that they had to call their own, which of course is a treasure when you have children. This was the only private place where they kept all the personal items, and they did not want us rummaging through their things, saying things like, "Look what I found." Over time, we grew to understand their reasoning and respect their privacy.

Having to ask someone to go into their personal space taught us to be aware of other peoples' boundaries and to have respect for their personal property. It also taught us that in life, we will not have access to everything and that not everything can be ours. It also taught us that other people will have things that have nothing to do with us and that we will have to respect that fact even if we don't like or understand it.

HOME TRAINED IN RESPECTING OTHER PEOPLE'S PROPERTY

Before overpriced prepackaged frozen foods were sold, many people purchased a huge freezer that was referred to as a deep freezer. It was looked at as a great investment because it allowed families to buy food in bulk at cheaper prices and then separate, repackage, and freeze the food themselves. Today, many companies have taken this idea and prepared frozen foods for their customers. Of course, this convenience comes with higher price tags, and not all companies list the date when the items were frozen, which makes it impossible to figure out how fresh they actually are. Some deep freezers were the size of a regular refrigerator and were usually stored in kitchens, garages, and basements; and others were slightly larger. People bought enough food from the store to last them at least an entire month. This process saved families a lot of money in the long run not only because it was cheaper to buy in bulk, but also because it helped them to prepare for each night's meal without having to continuously run back and forth to the grocery store for a little of this and a little of that—wasting time, money, and gasoline. As a child, it was fun to have a deep freezer around because we always knew there was something in there that we wanted to eat.

We were educated in many areas on how to save money whenever possible. We learned how to save by looking for deals at the store, buying in bulk, planning and preparing for dinners for the week, and not falling prey to options that offer us things that we are able to do for ourselves for free.

HOME TRAINED IN SAVING MONEY

It was very common for families to have their own gardens in the past. Even those who didn't have the biggest backyards may have still had a little section on the side of their homes where they planted their own fruits and vegetables. Fruit trees were also once a very popular sight before a home's view became more important than the fruit trees that were planted there. As children, we had so much fun picking berries, oranges, lemons, figs, cantaloupe, and other readily available fruits that we could snack on without having to run to the store or even in the house to enjoy. We also enjoyed picking fruit so that our family members could bake fresh cobblers, cakes, and pies. Having these gardens and trees ensured families that if they could provide nothing else; they would have always been able to provide food to eat. As I was becoming a teenager, it became "not cool" if your parents had a garden. People would say to us, "You mean your parents can't afford to buy those things at the store?" It didn't matter to my mother what people thought because she was happy to have her garden and felt that it was an asset to our family. Fresh fruit was the encouraging force that kept our diets regular and helped us out at snack time. Our parents never really had to figure out what our next snack would be because those trees were right there at our fingertips. It makes me wonder if it has become more popular to eat organic fruits and vegetables these days or more popular to buy them? In the days when buying organic foods are the most popular and most expensive, I am surprised that we do not see more gardens popping up all over the country in people's yards.

We learned that if all else fails and the prices at the grocery stores are raised too high, we can always feed ourselves by planting our own food.

HOME TRAINED IN PLANTING AND PICKING OUR OWN SEEDS OF HEALTH

"Cooking from scratch" and "home cooking" seem to be phrases from the past. Some young people do not know that *home-cooked* simply means that all of the meal ingredients were completely prepared at home. It's funny to hear people go on and on about the fact that they baked a cake from scratch based on the fact that they added the oil and eggs to the powder that came from the box. Although most of us have done that, it is important to teach the next generation that cooking from a box is not the same as cooking from scratch and that boxed foods were only created so that we would not have to spend the time creating something from scratch. It seems that kids always want the opposite of whatever they have and because my mother would never buy anything that came out of a box, we would always beg my mother to buy instant cake mix just so that we could see what it was about. She would say "I don't want that stuff in my kitchen," and we were teenagers before she gave in and allowed those boxed items to be brought into the house. What we found was that even though ready-to-mix-and-make meals may have been fun to make, they never tasted as good as my mom's recipes. In an instant society where people do not make time to do things in the same way that they used to, cooking from scratch has been thrown out of the shuffle along with many other things in many households. Although there are a lot of people who still prepare home-cooked meals, this way of cooking has taken on a negative association and become synonymous with the term *old-fashioned*. Prepackaged and preserved foods are loaded with ingredients that do not all properly break down in our systems. Because of this, many people suffer with health problems that they would love to now trade in for the time it would have taken to cook their foods from scratch.

We learned that instant foods were only supposed to be used as a quick fix, not as a permanent solution.

HOME TRAINED IN COOKING FROM SCRATCH

One of the first lessons that we learned about the kitchen, before we were taught how to cook, was how to grocery shop. Aside from the normal instructions of buying in bulk, cutting coupons, and buying items when they were on sale, we were also taught that every kitchen should always have staple items in the cabinets. When mentioning the words *staple items* to a lot of today's young adults, their immediate response is "Staples, what's that?" They have no idea what you're referring to and begin to question why office supplies would ever be kept in a kitchen. *Staples*, by definition, are foods that form the foundation of the diet of the people of a specific region. Years ago, foods that were the most commonly grown in a community were used the most and the most affordable, and therefore would be found in most people's kitchen. Foods like bread, rice, beans, pastas, and dairy products were considered staples in many areas and were always in our kitchen because from them alone, a filling meal could be made.

We learned how to utilize, prepare, and make the most out of the least. Having staples items in our kitchen taught us how to survive through the hard times.

HOME TRAINED IN UTILIZING STAPLES

Oftentimes, not having a certain ingredient to make a specific recipe made us test our creative side and create something new. Along with learning how to cook from scratch, we also learned how to make something great to eat out of what seemed to be nothing at all. Although we didn't have amazing cookbooks back then, we did have amazing meals. As little kids there were many times that we would look in the refrigerator and cabinets and think that there was no food in the house to eat and an hour or so later smell something cooking. We'd run to my mother and ask her where the food came from because when we looked we didn't see anything in the kitchen. She'd tell us that everything that was in the pot came from the same kitchen we looked in. It was then that we first began to pay attention to how to make something out of what seemed to be nothing at all. We learned that a few pieces of small vegetables and water could create a great broth and that a cup of rice mixed with those vegetable could make a nice soup. When asking older people to share their recipes, they sometimes can't remember exactly how much of a certain ingredient they used because they often just used however much they had. Because it was not always possible for them to run to a store for more of this or more of that, they made do with whatever was there, tasting their meals as they went along. The idea of making something out of nothing pushed us to figure out how to stretch one night's meal to last over the course of many nights. We learned how to turn the leftovers from one full chicken dinner into a second night of chicken and vegetables, a third night of chicken salad, and a fourth and fifth night of chicken soup. Not having recipes and only having ingredients has created some of the best chefs throughout the years because it forced them to think above the average thought.

We learned how to try new things and to make the best out of what we had.

HOME TRAINED IN MAKING SOMETHING OUT OF NOTHING

My parents were not very lenient with children who were self-proclaimed picky eaters. Aside from those of us who had food allergies, everyone else had to sit down and eat from the same meal. It was not normal then as it is now to hear a child constantly say "I don't want to eat that" because we ate whatever we were given. I have seen children recently watch their parents cook an entire meal for them but will still ask the question "Is there something else I can have instead of what you're making?" Interestingly enough, some parents respond by saying, "Well, let me see what I can make for you instead." When my children were toddlers and decided to ask that same question, I politely told them that their menu was on their plates. Our parents taught us at an early age that our kitchen was not a restaurant, and the food that we were given was for the health and nourishment of our body; and if by chance, one of our favorite meals was being served, we were in luck and should count it as a blessing. That helped us to understand that our parents were only feeding us so that we would not be hungry. It is important that children learn to appreciate the food that is given to them. Recognizing that food is for the health and nourishment of our bodies helped us to choose healthier foods once we were able to shop for ourselves.

We were taught to slow down and appreciate what was given to us and not be so quick to ask for the next best thing.

HOME TRAINED IN APPRECIATING OUR MEALS

By a certain time of the night after we ate dinner, the kitchen countertops were cleaned, and the lights that were lit for preparing a meal were turned off, even though there was no official sign, it always seemed as though our kitchen would be closed. We wandered in there for an occasional snack, but there was no all-night traffic where people were making new meals because typically we all ate around the same time. When my youngest child was about three years old, she never wanted to eat during our dinnertime. She would always say that she wasn't hungry when everyone else was eating dinner but would then start crying around midnight once she felt the hunger pains. The phrase "This is not a twenty-four-hour diner" was something that I would say to her to explain that my kitchen was not open twenty-four hours a day for her to eat and be served as she pleased. At first I felt sorry for her, but one day, when I knew she was not starving but was just going through her routine, I made her wait until the next morning to eat. From that day on, she ate with the rest of the family because she remembered how she felt the night before and knew that I was no longer going to play her game. She grew to understand that she needed to eat when dinner was being served and that I was not a waitress and would not be at her beck and call.

We were not allowed to run our parents schedule and were taught that time does not revolve around us.

HOME TRAINED IN UNDERSTANDING THAT OUR KITCHEN WAS NOT A TWENTY-FOUR-HOUR DINER

Because dinnertime was synonymous with family time, it was very important that everyone be present. However, as a teenager, if we choose to be somewhere else other than with our family during dinnertime—being over at one of our friends' house or busy doing some other activity that was not mandatory—it was up to us to make sure that we ate while we were out. We could not expect that everyone else was going to refrain from eating as much as he or she wanted just because we chose to be somewhere else. When our family sat down for dinner, everyone enjoyed himself or herself. There were times when we came home from hanging out to find that our favorite meal had been served, and we were left to make ourselves a sandwich. As soon as we were started complaining and asking "Why didn't anyone save me any?" my mom would say "There are no save-me-some-*s*" as a quick reminder that had we been eating with the rest of the family, we could have enjoyed the meal along with everyone else. If we were not there and by chance there were leftovers for us to enjoy, we considered ourselves lucky. However, it wasn't something that was to be expected. Of course, it was different if we were at a school function or something that was considered to be important. My mom would then always put a plate to the side for us.

This was another lesson learned in setting priorities and having consideration for other people. We learned to figure out what things were most important to us.

HOME TRAINED IN UNDERSTANDING THAT THERE WERE NO SAVE-ME-SOMES

Growing up, we were taught the value of cleanliness. We were pushed to see what a difference it made in our lives and over time learned to appreciate living in a house that was clean as opposed to one that was cluttered. Somewhere there must have been an unwritten list of the "responsibilities of a nine-year-old" because when I was around nine years old, my mother began teaching me how to wash, fold and iron clothes, wash dishes, clean the kitchen and the bathroom, and how to cook. Today, there are so many excuses used for why some parents have not taught their children how to do even the simplest household chores. Some say "They're too young" or "The window cleaner is too dangerous for them to use" or even "I do not want them to have to do the chores that I had to do when I was little" and opt to do it themselves or have a housekeeper run behind them. Although having a housekeeper can be a great help, it is very important that at the least everyone understands how to clean up after themselves incase they need to. Otherwise, our society will be full of young adults who do not know how to clean their own homes simply because no one ever took the time to show them how to do so properly. I was recently talking to a friend who has a housekeeper and she told me that even though her housekeeper comes to clean her home on a regular basis, her child's bedroom is never included in the job. She went on to tell me a story about the day when her son asked her why his room could not be included as well. She said that she laughed as she sat him down and explained to him that the housekeeper was being paid to come and take some of the load off her day due to the fact that she works hard and has a very busy schedule. However, given that children have more than enough time on their hands and should learn how to clean up after themselves, he needed to learn how to clean up after himself. This was something that she had intentionally set up this way so that her child would get into the habit of properly cleaning his room and understanding that cleaning up his mess is no one else's responsibility but his own. There were other little details that we learned about cleanliness like washing our towels and underwear before using them (there was a time when people actually washed towels and underwear *before* they used them). Today, many people think that it is odd to wash these items first because it takes up too much time. Something else that was said to be a big no-no for us was sitting on our beds with our "street clothes" or clothes that we played in outside on. We were allowed to play hard and get dirty but not allowed to then bring that dirt onto our beds where we laid our heads; we had to get cleaned up first. We were taught that we should keep the things that we keep close to our bodies like our comforters, sheets, and pillowcases clean, especially since these were all items that did not get washed every day. After we were all cleaned up and had changed into our lounge clothes or pajamas, we could then get comfortable and hang out and have fun on our beds. Keeping the walls clean from our little handprints seemed to be another processed point along our way, especially since a lot of people did not have the child-resistant, easy-to-clean glossy paint that we have today. We couldn't stand having to spend our day cleaning the walls, so instead we learned how to be mindful of what we put our hands on. I was recently in a deli with my daughter as she started leaning and putting her fingerprints on the glass. I had to stop and explain to her that someone had to clean that glass and that she was creating more work for someone else to have to do. She thought about it and from then on became more aware of how her actions could affect others.

We learned simple lessons about keeping things clean. Being a part of the cleanup process taught us to appreciate having a clean house and helped us to understand what was required to keep it that way.

HOME TRAINED IN THE VALUES OF CLEANLINESS

CHAPTER FIVE

The Makings of a Man

The Makings of a Man

Within this chapter live some of the great standard practices that were once poured into boys as they were growing up, in an effort to guide them into manhood.

STANDARD PRACTICES:

Building a man with love and confidence

Speaking a man into his existence

Properly introducing yourself by your full "Real" name

Thinking outside of the toy box

Everyone cannot make the team

Be a "Gentle" man

Be useful

Understanding the mentality of work boots vs. tennis shoes

Education is key

Learn how to take care of yourself

A man should always have money in his pocket

A half a loaf is better than no loaf at all

Go Hard or Go Home

Live off of what you have earned

The Dating Process

FIVE

Boys were at times loved in an equal but different way than girls. The love for a son seemed to come from taking the time to nurture him to have the confidence, strength, and ability to change the world. Many fathers and mothers made it a point to plant seeds of greatness into their sons at a very early age by not only teaching them how to do great things, but also by telling them how great they were so that when someone else said those same things to them, they would be able recognize it as being true. Even little boys were often referred to as Mommy's little man in an effort to teach them that they were going to grow up to be a man, which was said to them as a big deal. Years ago, many fathers chose not to display their affection for their sons through constant hugs and kisses but expressed their love through the personal time that they spent with them. The pats on the back and physical contact that came from playing sports and other games with them were treasured moments for many. Be it from hugs or playing games, boys appreciated having the love from both their mothers and fathers.

Many men learned how to love from the love that had been given to them. It was a gift that they were then able to share with their families. They were able to stand tall with the confidence that was planted into them as children.

STANDARD PRACTICE: BUILDING A MAN WITH LOVE AND CONFIDENCE

Because past generations recognized how significant language skills are in our society, communicating to children through baby talk was usually not encouraged after they reached a certain age, especially when it came to little boys. Once boys grew past their infant stages, many were no longer spoken to like babies but like the young men that they were being tailored into becoming. I remember hearing men tell the women in their lives "Don't talk to my son like a baby. He's growing up. Let him use his words." "Using his words" was considered essential because although many men could get a job that only required manual labor and no words at all, wanting to attain a high-level position required the proper use of words as a tool used to manage everyone else on the jobsite. In many cases, boys who had been spoken to like babies spoke in baby talk and were often teased by their peers. Boys were not only taught to use their words but to also speak with a confident tone in their voice, to always mean what they say, to say what they mean, and to look in the eyes of whoever they were talking to as a confirmation that their words were sincere and could be trusted. They learned that their words were their bond or connection to society and became a reflection on how they were viewed by others.

Boys were educated early on about the importance of having proper communication skills, which often gave them the confidence to succeed in other areas of their lives.

STANDARD PRACTICE: SPEAKING A MAN INTO HIS EXISTENCE

Years ago, a person's name was considered to be a big deal. People took pride in their family's last name as well as the first names that they gave to their children, especially when it came to boys. It was such a tradition to honor a little boy with someone else's first, middle, and last name. Many were either named after their fathers to continue their legacy, after one of their favorite family members in hopes that the child would take on that person's great traits, or were given a name that had great meaning in hopes that their child would grow into the meaning of that name. With this in mind, parents took the time to teach their children how to properly introduce themselves. Unlike today, in the past, when an adult asked a little boy "What's your name?" he would have never answered by saying "Mikey" or "Jay-Jay" but would have respectfully responded by saying "My name is Michael Smith" or "My name is Jason Reid." Children understood that their name and behavior was not only a reflection of themselves but also a direct link back to their family. People didn't always know all the children in the neighborhood, but if they knew their last name, they knew who their parents were or how to find them. I remember hearing kids introducing themselves many times and hearing someone else say "That's so-and-so's child." They didn't make the connection because they knew that child personally but rather because they recognized the last name and where the child was from. That association made kids think twice about acting up because even though everybody may not have literally known everybody else, people did pay attention to names. A man's name was ultimately viewed as the mirror image of his legacy. It was looked at as something similar to a "bowl of life." Everything that he did during his lifetime was put inside of his name. Leaving a legacy was viewed as something important that we grew to understand and respect.

Young men were taught that the reflection of who they were would always shine through their names and because of this were more mindful of what they did during their lives.

STANDARD PRACTICE: PROPERLY INTRODUCING YOURSELF BY YOUR FULL "REAL" NAME

While some boys had plenty of toy trucks and action figures to play with, others had none and were expected to "think outside of the toy box." In homes where toys were not overflowing, little boys were encouraged and given the opportunity to spend their time doing something that they found to be interesting. For many, not having traditional playthings helped to stretch their imaginations and open their minds wide enough to invent their own. Many would sit outside by themselves or with their friends and make toys from pieces of plastic, tree branches, and anything else that was nearby. One way that boys often became familiar with nature was by playing with bugs and other creatures that they found fascinating. Today, many are not being persuaded to explore nature in the same manner that they were years ago; but back in the days, if something wasn't poisonous, it was fair game to play with it. Unfortunately, many of today's boys do not even go outside to discover the possibilities or play with other kids in the neighborhood but instead sit inside the house and play video games and watch television to no end. Because of this, many are growing up with no real social skills and without the patience to sit and pay attention to anything that is not moving around on a screen. Some are even learning how to communicate with girls by the interaction that they see between men and women on television shows or on music videos rather than by actually going outside and just interacting with the girls who are around them. When the extremities of an imagination are brought to a child through video games and television, it lessens the likelihood of them wanting to think beyond what they have already seen.

Boys who had the ability to make toys and find friends usually carried those skills with them throughout their lives. They were typically the men who were inventive and creative, who used their imagination with whatever was given to them. Not having what seemed to be the norm gave many a greater appreciation for those special things that were given to them.

STANDARD PRACTICE: THINKING OUTSIDE OF THE TOY BOX

When I was growing up, most neighborhoods had their own football, basketball, and baseball teams that were usually made up of any of the neighborhood kids who decided that they wanted to play ball regardless of whether or not they had any skills that applied to the game. However, there were also teams that were considered to be the official teams in the community and were run through the school and park programs. In order to be on one of the official teams, it was mandatory that everyone go through the same tryout process and wait to be selected. Coaches chose the team players based on the number of spaces that were available and the skill set of the child in comparison to the other players. Today, some parents argue that children should never be made to try out for anything that they are interested in being a part of because having to face any kind of rejection is not fair and does not feel good. This way of thinking is understandable at the elementary school level when younger children have a harder time dealing with their feelings and understanding the logic behind the process. However, as children get older, it is important that they are able to understand the purpose of the process itself. Having to apply and try out for something forces kids to take the time to think about and make decisions on what they feel is worth their time and effort. It winds up being a great foreshadower and introduction of the reality of dealing with the competitiveness of life. Lessons like this teach kids to understand and come to grips with the fact that other people around them will often want the same things out of life that they want and may get them faster than they do. The focus, practice, and determination that this process requires are preparation for life's challenges and teach lessons on facing disappointment during the times when someone does not make the team. When a child does not make the team it forces them to decide whether or not what they think that they want is actually something that is worth trying out for again or if they feel that they will be better suited to do something else. Times of disappointment help them to redirect their greatness toward something else or to sharpen their pencil and get better. Helping children focus and work hard toward the things that they are interested in, congratulating them during their successes, and allowing them to go through their disappointments have a huge impact on how they deal with life's ups and downs in their adulthood.

The tryout process helped with the job interview process and even with things as simple as waiting to hear back on an invitation for a date.

STANDARD PRACTICE: EVERYONE CANNOT MAKE THE TEAM

Gentleness was a very important ingredient that was poured into the makings of a man. Ironically, being a gentle-man was synonymous with being strong enough to take the weight off of another person's load simply out of pure kindness and consideration. A few subtle ideals that reminded boys to think about the needs of others were instilled in them as they were encouraged to do things like offering to give up their seat so that someone else could sit down, opening a door or pumping gasoline for a woman just so that she did not have to do it and coming to the defense of someone's honor. They learned the significance of giving up their seat to any woman or elderly person who was standing nearby from the older men around them who always did the same thing. Over time, this helped them to open their minds and understand that helping others was very important. Opening a door for a woman was another courteous thing that young men were taught to do as a simple way of letting her know that he was looking out for her. This practice was once something that was very much appreciated. Not until recent years has there become such a big issue over whether or not women still want men to open doors for them or if they would prefer to do it themselves. It must have been in my teenage years that I remember it being the norm for women to pump their own gasoline. Before then, even though many women knew how to do it, they just didn't and either went through the full-service side of the gas station and had one of the attendants pump it for them, or it was done by one of the men in their lives. When boys learned these lessons at an early age, they became a part of what they viewed as normal and a great part of who they were. Because it was also expected that a man would stand up for and defend the honor of his mother, sisters, grandmothers, or any of the other women in his family in times of trouble, people were a bit more careful about how they treated women and thought twice about doing or saying something offensive to them out of the fear that someone in their family would come forward on the woman's behalf. If we lived by this type of thinking today, more people would be less comfortable in doing wrong because they would expect that someone would come to the rescue and stand up for what is right. Although chivalry is not completely dead, it seems to be dying at a very rapid pace.

These lessons taught boys to be kind and considerate to the people around them.

STANDARD PRACTICE: BE A "GENTLE" MAN

Years ago, whenever someone started a sentence with the expression "That no good, good for nothing" they were about to start talking about a man who never made any effort to be of help or use to anyone or any situation in need. These were the men who, no matter what they were asked to do, always seem to have an excuse about why they could not help. They were always too tired to do things like take out the trash and couldn't ever quite figure out how the lawn mower worked, and they didn't keep a job because, for whatever reason, every employer they ever worked for "didn't like or understand them." The reason why these men seemed to stick out and be the exception to the norm was because most boys were taught to be useful. Although they may not have been formally trained in areas like painting, changing tires, or fixing things around the house, they were constantly trying to figure out how something worked and how they could make something better. They didn't always have the money to pay someone else to have these things done for them, but because they had a strong will, they found a way. In many cases, at the point that a man realized that he was able to do some thing on his own, he refused to pay to have someone else to do it for him even if he had the money. Going through trials and efforts taught men many new things along the way. Back in the day, they were encouraged to learn how to do things like change the oil in their wife's car; and even those who never learned how to do it themselves would still take the car to be serviced so that their wife did not have to worry about it. At some point in history when women started demanding equal rights, some men felt that what they were really saying was that they no longer needed the men in their lives to do all the helpful things that they had done for them before; and that was just not true. It is important that young men understand that even though a woman has the right to do things for herself, it doesn't necessarily mean that she wants to. Many young women today complain of how frustrating it is to be in a relationship and have a life partner but have to do everything for themselves.

Young men were taught to understand that being useful or having an "I will try to help with whatever is needed" attitude is something that women are attracted to and greatly respect. They were shown the value in being helpful and how having initiative can be beneficial to them.

STANDARD PRACTICE: BE USEFUL

Shoes, as simple as they are, have become very symbolic of the mentality of many young men today in regard to how they feel about hard work. Years ago, it was not uncommon to walk into someone's house and see a pair of dirty work boots that had been left at the door. Even those men whose jobs did not require that they wear work boots usually still owned a pair and wore them whenever they did yard work around their house. In the past, men had no problem doing dirty work because they understood how they would benefit from their labor. Today, there are some who refuse to get themselves, their clothes, or their shoes dirty. Being well-groomed has always been important, but several men today are overly concerned. Casual tennis shoes have become more popular than ever before. Songs have even been written recently whose lyrics are about nothing else other than how important it is for a man to been seen in a brand-new pair of clean tennis shoes. One writer goes so far as to say that he never wears one pair of tennis shoes more than once, insinuating that if he did, they would not be as clean as they could be. The fact of the matter is that the only way someone could make sure that their shoes do not get dirty is to literally sit around and do nothing. This type of thinking is why so many boys today do not want to go outside and play or do household chores like taking out the trash, mowing the lawn, or washing the car out of fear of getting themselves dirty. Boys these days are reminded through so many areas of the media to stay "so fresh and so clean" while always "popping collars" instead of ironing collars and working hard. This mind-set pushes young men to feel as though having only one pair of shoes is not enough, which in many cases brings down their levels of appreciation for what they do have. It is unfortunate that there has not been an outburst of pride put into songs about wearing work shoes. When you think about the fact that tennis shoes were created so that people would have a shoe to play in but have now become the most important shoes to own in the eyes of children, it should make us question the message that we are sending to our young men. Many are now trying to figure out how to earn enough money to have so many pairs of play shoes without working hard enough to get them dirty. When young men have never been exposed to doing any type of "dirty work," if and when times should ever get hard and the only job offered to them to provide for their family is one that will get them dirty, their privileged mentality may make them hesitate to accept the offer rather than being grateful for the opportunity.

Young men were taught the value of working hard. Even though "work smarter and not harder" has become a very popular saying in our society and is great if you are able to do so, we have to remember to teach young people that there is nothing wrong with getting dirty or doing hard work if there is a need to do so.

STANDARD PRACTICE: UNDERSTANDING THE MENTALITY OF WORK BOOTS VERSUS TENNIS SHOES

When I was growing up, most people recognized that being educated was like having a key that opened up a life of possibilities for both boys and girls. Many children were encouraged to further their schooling beyond their high school years in order to be in a position to obtain a career that would help them to make the most out of their lives. However, during my grandparents' time, because there were no child welfare laws like there are now that required that parents send their children to school every day, a lot of boys were forced to drop out of school as early as in their elementary years so that they would have the time to go out, get a job, and help to support their families. When speaking to men who lived during that era, they all seem to bring up the conversation about how they saw firsthand the importance of having an education because in their days those who had not been given the opportunity to learn how to read properly seemed to struggle more than those who had. Some men stated that they were often ashamed and treated poorly because of their ignorance. The irony is that they did not choose to be ignorant and were smart enough to realize that they would much rather have learned how to read properly. Many who dropped out of school or were never allowed to go became the driving force that pushed their sons and grandsons to graduate from high school and college. They understood what effect not having a degree could have on the progression of one's life and the difference that it made in the lack of opportunities that were afforded to them. Older men often complain about how the youth of today, who are dropping out of school for no good reasons, take too many things for granted and have no idea what opportunities they are turning their backs on. Men who earned degrees also pushed their sons and grandsons to obtain degrees as well because they witnessed the difference an education made in their lives. An old classmate once said that his ability to read led him to study places in the world that were once only pictures in a book and that those pictures planted a desire in him to travel and see those places that he had once only read about. His desire to travel and learn more about the world gave him the motivation to finish school so that he could eventually get a job and be able to afford to go on those trips. That to me was a perfect example of the fact that you can only be or do what you know exists. Today, when moneymaking moguls are constantly emerging from what seems to be nowhere and a traditional education is not valued in the same manner that it once was, we have to make sure we teach our children that it is still very important that they gain the knowledge that they will need to be properly trained in whatever field they decide to go into. We have to make sure they understand that even though their ideas may be a big seller, if they do not understand the basics of business, they will never know how to manage their own success.

Men taught their sons that every generation should always do better than the last because they have access to gain more than those before them.

STANDARD PRACTICE: EDUCATION IS KEY

Because there used to be very traditional roles set within marriages, it was once expected that when a man married, his responsibility would be to work to provide for his family, and his wife's responsibility would be to manage many aspects of his life. She was said to make sure that his children were cared for, his house was clean, his meals were provided, and his clothes were washed, as well as other things that helped his home and life to function properly. Some men were married right out of high school and reaped these benefits early on. They went from living in their parent's home to living with their wife or girlfriend without ever learning anything about taking care of themselves. Those who had all their needs taken care of by their mothers, without learning how to do anything for themselves, eventually became another woman's burden. I've heard women today say things like "His mom did not teach him how to do anything for himself. I don't think that he was ever taught to even think to pick his clothes up off of the bathroom floor." Coming out of the olden days, some people considered cooking and cleaning to be women's work, but others saw teaching their sons how to do so as an opportunity to make sure they could handle taking care of themselves. These men were taught how to manage their finances, clean their homes, wash their clothes, cook for themselves, and take care of all of their other business as well. Although many looked forward to having a wife who could help them with these tasks, because they knew how to do these things on their own they did not just marry a woman because she knew how to do these things but because they loved her and wanted to be with them because of the connection that they shared. Now, more than ever, with marital roles continuously changing and the fact that many families can't afford for the wife to stay home and take on all the household tasks, it has become even more important that young men are taught how to take care of themselves. Giving a young man the tools or knowledge to eventually take care of himself is essential.

Young men were taught that although a woman can be of great help and add value to their lives, her help or the lack thereof should not take away from who they are as men as a whole.

STANDARD PRACTICE: LEARN HOW TO TAKE CARE OF YOURSELF

I remember hearing older men tell younger men that a man should always have money in his pocket. It was usually something that was said to them as they entered into the workforce—a phrase often used in an attempt to teach them that as men, they should always be able to provide for themselves. It was a subtle reminder that they should never spend all their money without having some portion of it saved and set aside for a later time. Men were taught that they should be able to stand tall and make solid decisions on their own and that by keeping money in their pockets or having a steady income, they would have the freedom to make those decisions without having to listen to anyone else's opinion. In those days, the quickest way to have people in your personal business adding their suggestions and advice to your life was by asking them for any kind of help, especially any type of financial assistance. A man who was able to keep a steady job, properly budget his finances, and provide for himself on a regular basis wasn't viewed as someone that needed anyone else's advice and was therefore highly respected. Those who sharpened these skills while they were single found it to be easier to apply what they had learned as they transitioned into being a husband and a family man. Unfortunately, there are men who have heard this saying but do not truly understand what it means. Somehow, somewhere along the way, the root of the phrase has gotten lost in translation. Some who have families today misunderstand this saying and think that because someone told them that a man should always have money in his pocket, they are to have one pocket filled with money for themselves and the other filled with money for their family. However, in tough economic times when there is only enough money to fill one pocket, what many don't understand is that they are supposed to include the money for themselves in with the money for their family. Once a man is married, he has to make sure that his family as a whole is taken care of first, and then, and only then, if there are extra funds available, he should indeed have those extra funds to do as he pleases.

This phrase gave young men an incentive to earn their own income so that they could provide for themselves.

STANDARD PRACTICE: A MAN SHOULD ALWAYS HAVE MONEY IN HIS POCKET

There was once a time when men were appreciative of employment opportunities that were offered to them. Little boys were taught that no one was required to *give* them a job and that they needed to check any negative attitudes that they may have had at the door before they walked in to an opportunity. It was a normal thing for a man to sit a boy down and tell him that if he ever was in search of a job and couldn't find "the right one" that would provide the salary that he was looking for, he ought to consider working two jobs in order to make up for the difference in salary. They were shown how working one, two, or even three part-time jobs, even if they weren't the most exciting positions, while they were looking for something that they enjoyed would put them in a much better situation than to have no job at all. They learned to always take the opportunities that they were *blessed* with until they could replace them with something better. Even the little boys in the neighborhood had odd jobs like mowing yards or delivering newspapers. They learned how to do a few things at one time until they found something that paid off big. A man once told me that his grandfather used to tell him that "a half a loaf is better than no loaf at all." This expression taught him to work hard and appreciate the opportunities that he could get his hands on. It also taught him about the importance of setting priorities in life. Today it seems crazy and unfortunate that so many young men feel that they are entitled to begin at the end of the last *s* in the word *success* or start at the top of everything that they apply for. Back in the day, many men were happy about having the opportunity to be hired as an apprentice or trainee, knowing that even though they would not receive a paycheck, they would be compensated with the knowledge, training, and good advice that would be handed down to them through the actual experience. This system was set up to help them realize that hard work and dedication toward anything eventually pays off and that having the knowledge it takes to do something will eventually become the power needed to manage it. Of course, they had the option to work on jobs that didn't require much training; but for those who really wanted a career in a particular field, taking the time to train and prepare while still working a couple of other jobs on the side until they were qualified to be paid for their services was more important. I hear young men these days say "I don't want to take a second job," but the fact of the matter is that the men of yesterday didn't want to take a second job either. However, they put their priorities in order and decided that they had no alternative but to continue to work as many jobs as they needed to so that their families could survive while they prepared for their next step. Not everything could be a priority. If it meant that they had to walk to work to save on gas money so that their kids could have decent shoes, then that is what they did. Most men of yesterday didn't quit their jobs before they found another because it didn't make sense back then; and although it doesn't make sense today either, for some reason, it has become a popular thing to do. Women were supportive and had a lot of understanding, but they also understood that a man who didn't have a job was a man who spent his days looking for one. There weren't many jobs that were considered to be "not good enough" for a man who did not have one. They knew how to pick up their pride and put it to the side when necessary. There was a time when it meant more for a man to have his family be proud that he was providing for them by working at a grocery store as a janitor than be embarrassed in front of his friends for taking that same job. The phrase "half a loaf is better than no loaf at all" was important because it emphasized the fact that a half can still be divided, but when there is no loaf at all, everyone goes hungry.

This phrase was used to help teach young men how to be a true team player and understand that their team, or family, may need them to take a job that they may not be interested in but is the only job available to help provide for their family at the time.

STANDARD PRACTICE: A HALF A LOAF IS BETTER THAN NO LOAF AT ALL

"Go hard or go home" was an expression that retired men seemed to use whenever talking about their days in the workforce. They'd sit around talking to each other for hours on end about how hard they worked during their time and how the men in the current day would never be able to relate because they don't have the experience to "know anything about it." They would say that their labor and efforts, regardless of whatever job they were hired to do, were never less than what was required because of the pride that they put into their work. They never wanted anybody to be able to say anything bad about something that they worked on. At one point in time, a lot of men were brick masons by profession, whose job it was to build many of the brick walls and chimneys of so many buildings that still exist today. They had to be very precise and pay close attention to details as they created straight and level structures that were seen by many. The presentation of a man's work in those days was a representation of his character. If he paid attention to detail in his work, it was assumed that he paid attention to the details in the other aspects of his life as well. But if he was careless in his work, he was typically viewed as someone who was careless in how he handled his personal life. The older generation would stress to the young boys coming up behind them that if they decided that they were going to do something, they should either do it to the best of their ability or not do the work at all. They'd ask questions like "Why would you come to work and embarrass yourself when you could have stayed home and done that?" A number of jobs required a lot of teamwork, and sometimes a day's pay for the entire team depended on the completed day's work. There was no time in the middle of a job to waste, and some teams had no patience for a man who did not do his part. The last person that a group of hardworking men wanted to be on their team was a man who was not willing to work hard and was weighing them down. They learned to either show up to work hard or that they could be sent home.

Young men were taught to work hard, do a great job, and take pride in their work; they were encouraged to get more out of their jobs than just their paychecks. Working hard within a group or department created a sense of unity and helped them as individuals to see the importance of being a team player.

STANDARD PRACTICE: GO HARD OR GO HOME (WORK ETHICS)

"Live within your means" was just another way of saying "Don't spend more money than you earn." There were times when families didn't have enough money for everything that they may have wanted or needed, and although a lot of people shared whatever they had as a community, many men were too proud to ask anybody for help beyond necessity. They would tell their sons that a man should always be able to take care of his family and that if he learns to live and be content with what he already has; it will make things a lot easier for him in the long run. It was said to be okay to ask for help if and only if there was a real need, but a man should never ask someone for help to get things in life that are considered to be extra. If he wanted more, he was encouraged to make a plan and figure out how to earn more, but that in situations where having more was not an option, he had to learn how to be comfortable and satisfied with what he had. Even though credit was not accessible then in the same manner that it is today, many were against the concept altogether. It was hard for some to understand why some one would be willing to go into debt over things that were not essential. It was considered one thing to have a running bill or line of credit at the neighborhood general store in order to buy groceries or toiletries for your family. However, it was something else altogether to have a running bill at a department store for clothes that were purchased but not needed. Now, today, as a society, we tend to live off credit cards and reap the benefits of unearned labor in hopes to one day pay off our debt.

Having to earn their keep *or work for the things wanted before they were able to be purchased helped us all to make clearer decisions on what items we felt were worth our hard-earned money.*

STANDARD PRACTICE: LIVING OFF WHAT YOU HAVE EARNED

There were certain things that most young men were taught to view as general principles of dating. Of course, being a respectful gentleman was high on the list of standards. They were reminded to respect their dates in the same manner that they would like for a man to respect their mother, sister, or daughter. When they were caught saying something inappropriate to a girl, they would usually be asked, "Now is that how you would want someone to talk to your sister?" When picking a young lady up to take her out on a date, out of respect for her as well as her family, a man was expected to get out and introduce himself, let her family know where he would be taking her, and have her home by a respectable time. No matter how *grown-up* a couple thought that they were, as long as they lived in their family's home, they were expected to be back in the house at whatever was considered to be a decent hour. Boys were taught to be courteous toward women and to look out for their well-being. They were taught to protect the woman who they were with. I remember walking down the street with my dad, and I must have been about four years old, and hearing him say to me that I was walking on the wrong side of the sidewalk. He went on to tell me that a man should always walk on the outside of the sidewalk closest to the street whenever walking with a lady in an effort to protect her from possible harm. Many young men were taught the importance of being able to make smart, solid decisions on their own without having to first get an approval from their mothers because most women did not want to date what was considered to be a *mama's boy*, and if the relationship ever became serious, it would be necessary for him to be able to lead his family in the right direction. One of the most important rules in dating was that a man needed to be able to provide for himself before he could provide for a girlfriend, a wife, or a baby. Some complain about the costs that are related to dating but need to understand that the costs related to taking a woman out on a date are just a small reflection of what it really means to provide for a family. Old men used to say things like "If you can't take care of her now, don't put yourself in a position where you'll have to take care of her later." The same thought applied to those young men who, although they didn't really love the young lady who they were dating, were putting themselves in situations that could tie them to her for the rest of their lives. Although music and television has a tremendous influence on our youth, we must be there to take the time to talk to them and explain the truths and consequences about certain things that they are being exposed to.

Many young men were allowed to travel through the dating process with the freedom to experience it but with the guidance to understand it.

STANDARD PRACTICE: THE DATING PROCESS

CHAPTER SIX

The Pieces of a Woman

The Pieces of a Woman

This chapter reveals some of the "pieces" or key things that were given to us as little girls to use as building blocks as we moved toward womanhood. They helped us to develop into respectful, kind, and confident women.

IMPORTANT PIECES:

Learning how to love yourself

Understanding that "Beauty is in the eye of the beholder"

Understanding that "Pretty is as pretty does"

Appreciating your age

Modesty

Staying out of harm's way

Learning about the Dating Process

Displaying appropriate affection

Being aware of and respecting your own image

Understanding how to properly maintain a household

Being loving towards others

SIX

When I was a little girl, the reflection of the love that my family gave to me became the blueprint of how I learned to love others. The underlined confidence that they instilled taught me that it was also okay for me to love myself as well. My parents made sure that we knew how important we were and reminded us that we were special and were loved on a regular basis because they wanted us to be able to recognize that "special something" within ourselves. Understanding this prevented me from falling into the hands of the first little boy who told me that he thought I was special or the first man that told me that he loved me. This was an amazing piece of information for me to understand as I started dating because it helped me to narrow down those things that I looked for within a relationship. It made me understand that because I already had my family's love in my life, I could enjoy love when I found it rather than spending my time searching for someone to give me something that I'd never had. Through this, I learned that there was no need to look for someone to validate who I am as a person or supply me with a great love of self because my parents had already colored in the lines of that picture. Instead, I found excitement in finding a true connection and friend who I enjoyed spending my time with, who shared my same interests. Many of us in relationships, both young and old, get excited when new things that we have never experienced are presented to us. Whether it's love and attention or material items, we sometimes pay more attention to those *things* rather than how we are being treated overall. Because of this way of thinking, a friend once said that he gave his seven-year-old daughter a ring and told her that the ring symbolized the love and support that he promised to always show her. He said that he did this so that she could feel what a true commitment felt like over time and wanted her to know what to expect when a man offered her a ring of commitment. He, like my parents, didn't want his daughter's perception—when looking to see if there was true love within a relationship—to be clouded by gifts given out of manipulation. It is important that little girls are shown true love as they grow up so that being loved becomes a natural part of their lives rather than something new that they have to try and find and do the most to hold on to.

We learned the value in loving ourselves.

AN IMPORTANT PIECE: LEARNING HOW TO LOVE YOURSELF

Growing up in a family where there were so many girls who all carried their own unique sense of style and beauty forced us to deal with our personal issues of self that related to our differences. We each had our own perception of what we considered to be beautiful and oftentimes, as with many little girls, felt that it was the opposite of whatever we had been given. Whether it was the size of our noses, the length of our hair, the shape of our bodies, or any other issue that related to our self-image, most of us at one point or another had moments when we felt insecure. I will never forget feeling bad one day about how I looked in comparison to someone else. My mother sat me down and said, "BeNeca, you are beautiful to me but must know that you are beautiful for yourself. You should also be aware that true beauty is in the eye of the beholder, which means that how beautiful you are to other people is always going to be subjective to who is looking at you at that time, and since you will always be looking at yourself first, you should find your own beauty and feel good about who you are." She went on to tell me that I needed to take the time to identify those things that I found to be beautiful about myself but also celebrate what I thought was weird or unusual because those were the special things that God had given to me that made me different from everybody else. I learned how to appreciate, embrace, and enhance those special things so that they would shine rather than be hidden. Through this, I learned how to accept the fact that everyone will not think that I am the most beautiful person; but just as I found beauty within myself, someone else would find beauty in me as well. Once I started dating, this lesson helped to ease my pain when finding out that the person who I was interested in was interested in someone else. I learned that certain people like certain things and that I shouldn't be offended by that. Self-esteem often builds the bridge of confidence that little girls need when looking for their own special something.

We learned to love and identify with what made us uniquely beautiful.

AN IMPORTANT PIECE: UNDERSTANDING THAT BEAUTY IS IN THE EYE OF THE BEHOLDER

There is something so lovable about the sweetness of little girls that makes most people fall in love with them and feel that they can do no wrong. When we were little, we sometimes tried to use our cuteness as leverage to get us out of trouble. Batting our eyes and smiling big worked on some of our family members but not with my mother. No matter how lovely we thought we were, if we started acting up, we were likely to hear her tell us that "pretty is as pretty does," followed by instructions to not act ugly. This subtly reminded us that a person's true beauty blooms from within. I can remember seeing some women who had gorgeous facial features but wondering what happened to them because they were not attractive people. It was obvious that they were once very pretty, but their beauty was hard to fully capture because they wore their attitudes on their faces. We were warned that pretty women who do ugly things will literally turn into ugly women. This made me mindful that my expressions and emotions could literally, over time, mold onto my face. For my own selfish reasons, this logic made me think twice about doing the wrong things out of fear that it would show in my appearance.

We discovered that no matter how pretty *someone may be, beauty can be worn down by someone's actions and lifestyle.*

AN IMPORTANT PIECE: UNDERSTANDING THAT PRETTY IS AS PRETTY DOES

"Get your hands off of your imagination" was a phrase that was said to us as little girls whenever we started to say something but felt the need to put our hands on our hips and sway our bodies from side to side as though we thought it made us look like we were grown women. The word *imagination* was used as a quick metaphor to remind us that what we were trying to act out was about as real as our imagination. We were often encouraged to enjoy every step and every stage of our lives to the fullest. I can remember hearing older people say, "Don't grow up too fast," telling us to enjoy where we were because our lives would pass us by so quickly. It seems that many people never pay attention to their present stage in life. They often only look to the future as they watch their lives go by in a backward slideshow of photographs. Because of this, I decided to start taking my life's photos with my eyes, wide open, instead of my camera every step of the way. I made a decision to allow the good and bad times in my life to soak in so that I could fully remember them with no desire to go back and relive those moments. As children, we were taught that life has certain cycles that most people will go through at one point or another. We were reminded that many people who act fifty at fifteen go on to act fifteen at fifty in order to fulfill their own cycle of life, but that if we take life one bite at a time and fully digest it, we'll always feel full and have no regrets.

This helped us to appreciate our age, living each moment to the fullest.

AN IMPORTANT PIECE: APPRECIATING YOUR AGE

Modest was once a word that was often used when describing how a woman or a girl presented herself to and around other people. It is synonymous with the word *reserved*, which to us was an important parallel because *reserved* means "to place something to the side for the right time or the right person," and that is exactly what we were encouraged to do with ourselves. Our parents set certain standards about modesty that they then planted in to the seeds of our character. Many of these standards were based around how we carried ourselves as well as the clothes that we wore. One of the first things that most little girls from my day learned about getting dressed was that, for the exception of very few situations, we should always be dressed. It was never considered cute for us to run around the house naked. By the time we could actually run, we were already being taught the value of having self-respect. I learned that being naked was not a bad thing but that I just did not need to be naked in front of other people. One of our house rules was that whenever we got out of the bathtub or shower, we were to get dressed in at least our robe or pajamas before coming out of the bathroom. My mother never seemed to stop finding ways to guide us in the right direction. Lessons on modesty were slid into things as simple as instructions on when to wear pajama pants rather than nightgowns. Usually, we were free to wear whatever we wanted to wear to bed. However, because we were active girls who played a lot, we wore pajama pants instead of nightgowns when our parents had male company in our home because it allowed us to play more freely. However, looking back on it—unless we were saying our good nights—we were hardly ever in the same room as our parents' company once it was bath—and bedtime. My mom taught us that even though we would never be able to control another person's actions, it was important that we were mindful of our own. She made sure that we had a clear understanding that there were some things that we could do in certain situations but not in all, that might help us to stay out of harm's way. This helped us to become more conscious of our surroundings, and reminded us to carry ourselves in a particular way. A key rule of dressing modestly for us as little girls was always wearing shorts underneath our skirts and dresses. Although we were not encouraged to play hard and flip around and upside down while wearing skirts or dresses, our parents knew that no matter what, as children, we would always be tempted. Because of this, we were made to wear these shorts so that if we forgot what we were wearing and started playing really hard, our underclothes would not be seen. Even with shorts on, I can still hear my aunt say, "You know you have on a skirt right?" or being told, "Don't make me have to remind you that you have on a dress."

The only exception to the "shorts rule" was if we were wearing stockings; and that was only because if we had stockings on, we were too dressy to be flipping upside down anyway. We grew to understand that our bodies are our temples and should always be viewed as something special to be cherished and reserved for revealing and sharing only at the right time and with the right person. Wearing slips underneath our dresses and skirts was something else that was once mandatory for us to have on when we weren't wearing shorts. Slips were worn to prevent people from being able to see through our clothes and so that our panty lines would not bring extra attention to our behinds by showing through our clothes. Somewhere along the way, thong panties replaced slips. Unfortunately, the thong not only physically replaced the slip, but it also mentally replaced the modesty that was embedded in it. Of course, at a certain age boys will be boys, but slips helped to push their imagination back a little further from the immediate reality of the essence of our bodies. The slip, for little boys, was like reading a cartoon strip and imagining the scenes being played out in live action, whereas the thong allows the body to move in 3-D. Unlike all the images that boys see firsthand today, the slip left something to their imaginations. It was a big deal for a young man to say to his friends, "Man, I saw her slip." Even though we were taught that no one had the right to bother us regardless to what we were wearing, we also learned that we should be the first and best example of someone who respects our body. The mind-set of being modest helped us to understand that we should never give too much of ourselves away too quickly. It made us realize that we did not need to bring special attention to our bodies and that true sexiness is when beauty and humility come together and are seen without having to be announced. My mother used to say when speaking to us about our bodies, "A nice figure will show through a paper bag or regardless of what you're wearing." She'd also tell us that there is no need to advertise goods that are not being sold. Needless to say, we weren't allowed to wear tight, short, low-cut, or any other clothing that was revealing in any way. It's interesting how our fashion sense in society is led by what "other people" who we do not even know are saying is best. I am always surprised when I hear people say that they don't like the way that their daughters dress, but there is nothing that they can do because society is pushing them to do something different from what they agree with even though they are the people who are buying the clothes. It makes me wonder if that is just what they are saying but that they really like their daughters to look the way they do. Unlike today, when I was growing up, little girls who were dressed up to look just like their mothers were not seen as anything to brag about. Just like with women, little girls' attitudes are greatly affected by what they wear. Nowadays, many mothers seem to think that it is the cutest thing for their daughters to look just like they do; dressing them in miniskirts, high heels, half shirts, lipstick, and nail polish. It makes one wonder if these mothers may have stopped playing with dolls too soon. Some do not realize how these things affect their daughter's self-perception. I have found that the best example of this is to watch little girls when they play dress up. Their whole attitude changes when they start "playing grown-up," which is never a problem when they are in their homes and are able to recognize that this is all just *make-believe* at that stage in their lives. The problem occurs when they carry that attitude away from the play area or when their parents encourage this behavior beyond playtime. This same problem often occurs at the preteen and teenage stages. However, at this age—although they are still playing grown-up—the makeup, hair extensions, and clothing are all items that real women use so they tend to be a bit more confused about their lines of reality. Today when girls are developing at a faster pace and appear to be grown women, they are being approached by grown men at an earlier age. This is often when the lines of make-believe cross over into the reality of looking and *acting* like a woman even when you are still a child. When a little girl is dressed inappropriately and starts prancing around like she is just as grown as her mother, it should be no surprise when her attitude begins to change. It still amazes me when I go to a nail salon how many toddlers are having their nails done. What happened to having something to look forward to? The hair salon, although occasionally necessary for special occasions and deep conditioners, is no longer being taught to be a *treat* but rather something that *is expected* by many children. We were taught how to comb our hair and keep ourselves clean and groomed as kids. We were required to wear our hair in braids, plats, and ponytails until we were so old that it looked awkward. This wasn't just because it was the easiest thing to do, but it also served an entirely different purpose as well. Our appearance made it very clear to us as well as to grown men that no matter how tall we were, *we were children.* However, today, some people run from that old-school theory and say to their stylist, "Please style my daughter's hair because if I have to do it myself, she won't look as nice." When you couple that type of thinking with the adult-like clothing worn, high-heeled shoes, manicures, and pedicures, it makes you wonder where there is room left for the child. With all of the things to spend money on today, why people are spending so much on unnecessary things for their children that teach them the wrong message or no message at all and could possibly put them in danger is something that is hard to understand.

Learning about modesty helped us to fully understand the concept of respecting ourselves. It taught us to take pride in our bodies beyond the level of displaying what they looked like. It also taught us that in relationships, we do not have to give everything to our potential partners in advance.

AN IMPORTANT PIECE: MODESTY

My parents realized early on that they would not be able to be there by our side to protect us all the time. Because of this, there were certain conversations that they had with us about life, people, and situations, especially for us girls that opened up our sense of awareness and helped to keep us safe. My mother was really big on preventing *misunderstandings* from happening. One conversation that I remember clearly happened one day when my mom pulled me to the side and told me that I was not allowed to sit on any man's lap. This wasn't something that was constantly talked about but something that was definitely understood. As a child, I had no idea why this was so important; but as I got older, I learned that everyone's intentions are not always the best. Although we were very close to the men in our lives and were always being picked up and given hugs and kisses, there was no way you could make my mom understand why it was ever necessary for us to sit on a man's lap as a term of affection. She never wanted to hear someone tell her that what she saw him doing wasn't what it looked like in regard to her daughters. Once we were beyond our toddler years, we did not even sit on our father's lap. Because children can sometimes have a hard time explaining certain things to the adults who they respect, my mother felt that if we could explain to any man that insisted that we sit on his lap that we were big girls who did not even sit on our father's lap anymore, they would not be able to express any anger or be offended. She explained to us that it only takes one time and one experience, especially when children are too young to express the things that have happened to them, for someone to do something wrong that would affect our lives. It was better to prevent a problem, when possible, than to try to fix it later.

This was a lesson that taught us about keeping ourselves out of harm's way as much as we knew how. Although we did not understand it initially, as we got older, we understood how we were to apply this same theory to other scenarios in our lives.

AN IMPORTANT PIECE: STAYING OUT OF HARM'S WAY

Looking back on how we were introduced to dating made me realize how many stages were developed for us and how much of a process it actually was. Because our parents recognized that there were certain aspects of life that we would eventually venture in to, they decided to introduce us to those things and let us move forward according to what they thought we could handle while still watching over us as much as they felt that we needed them to. Today, when talking about speaking to teenagers about dating, the focus seems to be more so on preventing childbirth rather than how to develop age-appropriate relationships. Before we were allowed to go on one-on-one dates with boys, we were encouraged to go on Saturday outings with groups of friends to places like the movies or bowling alleys because this allowed us to get the feel of being out socially without being in an exclusive setting. Even after we were permitted to have more personal time with our date, our parents were still involved in the process and dropped us off and picked us up to and from wherever we were going during the daytime hours. Eventually, we were given the green light to go out at night on official dates but still lived within certain boundaries that were set by our parents. Dating was a really big step during our teenage years. This was when we learned so many of the dos and don'ts of being respected within a relationship. One of those boundaries was our curfew, and coming home after curfew was an enormous deal. We were expected to be home by whatever time our parents set as our curfew. If our parents told the young man that we were going out with that we were to be home by 9:00 p.m. and we came home at 9:15 p.m., our curfew would then be reversed and reset to 8:45 p.m. to remind us that they were not playing around with what they said. I remember one night when my cousin who was eighteen and living at home at the time decided that she was going to come home at 3:00 a.m. one more time . . . in spite of her mother's warnings. On this particular evening, my aunt had had enough of pacing back and forth, wondering whether or not her child was in harm's way or just still hanging out with her boyfriend. She decided that it was time that her daughter learned a really valuable lesson and was given a quick glimpse of what her reality could be. She packed her daughter's suitcases and sat them outside on the front porch. When my cousin—who thought she was just going to quietly sneak in—arrived at the house, she was startled to see many of her things sitting outside. It finally dawned on her that her mother was no longer going to be up worrying about her well being while she was out having fun. As she walked up to the house, my aunt came outside and asked her boyfriend to wait there until she could get all her things ready for him to pack up and take with him. She told them that since neither one of them could figure out how to respect her household or her house rules, he must have had plans to move her out in to his house and take care of all her needs. Needless to say, after a long night's conversation, that was the last time that ever happened. Many older parents and grandparents had a house rule that stated that no one was allowed to leave or come in to their house after a certain time. They were not going to be awakened at all times of the night by someone coming in at all hours. I had a friend in my twenties who was told by her grandmother who she lived with that if she didn't make it into the house by a decent hour, she expected her to stay wherever she was until the next day. However, if she didn't come home too many times, it was understood that she was preparing and getting ready to start looking for her own home.

Not only did we have a set curfew to follow when going out on a date, but there were only certain types of places that our parents considered to be appropriate for us to be taken to. Late nights out at the beach or other secluded areas were off-limits. As girls, our parents wanted us to be taken to public places where we could be seen and have witnesses to whatever was going on. Even after being given the okay to date, we still had to earn the opportunity to be able to have an official boyfriend. It was not something that was a right given to us by age but by our level of maturity based on how we handled the other mandatory requirements in our lives. If we were able to carry ourselves like respectable young women, were smart enough to manage our school—and homework, and were at least of a certain age, our parents considered letting us socialize with young boys our own age with a more concentrated focus. It wasn't like it is today when many parents think it is the cutest thing to say that their child has a boyfriend or girlfriend at the age of five years old. Some seem to be filling their children's heads with thoughts to start looking for someone to call their own before they can properly read but then wonder why their children are getting into trouble at school doing things that a boyfriend would be doing to his girlfriend and vice versa rather than focusing on their schoolwork. With all that we had to fill our minds with, thoughts of boyfriends were nowhere near what we were being guided to be thinking about as a young child. Once we were allowed to officially have boyfriends, it was considered to be a big deal to our family as a whole. Of course there have always been people who snuck around dating folks who their families considered being the *wrong* person for them to be with; but for many, it was a process that everyone wanted to be a part of. I grew up in a family where I had a large number of older uncles and male cousins who made it very clear when I was about to start dating, that it was extremely important that they met any young man that I was interested in going out with before I officially started dating him. They wanted to have the opportunity to invite him over and get to know his viewpoint on life as well as his intentions in dating me. They felt that it was necessary to find out what he considered "normal ways of life" and, at the same time, wanted to make sure that he understood what matters my family valued. My folks wanted to meet his folks or at least his parents so that for one, there were no secrets about the fact that he was dating me; and two, they wanted to get a glimpse of where he came from. Even in families where there weren't a lot of people to serve as a protecting force, it was once still important that a young man understood that there was someone who would hold him accountable for a young woman's well-being while she was in his care. There was a time when men would sit young women in their family down just as they were about to start the dating process and give them some tips or insights on basic things about men. I remember being told in random conversations things like "Even though you may be attracted to someone and have a lot of fun with them, you need to understand that long-term relationships require a lot more than just that" or "Most men want a woman who just gets (or understands) them without having to constantly justify the rationale behind their feelings; and although there are things that a couple can get to know about each other through daily conversation, when two share a similar upbringing, it can sometimes make it easier for them to build something together based on their previous foundation." Their talks with me taught me that a lot of who a man is, is built from his past experiences, and if he has to overly explain or justify why he feels a certain way about everything all the time to his mate, it makes it harder for him to be able to truly relax. But if a woman understands his experiences because they were a part of her experiences as well, they may be able to relate to each other better. This taught me that it's great to be with someone who adds new things to my life that I can learn from, but having certain things in common and being like-minded in certain areas can really help with the flow of the relationship. Along with all the info that was given to us about dating, we were also given a speech on understanding the importance of always making sure that someone knew where we were going and who we were going with. Letting someone know our whereabouts was just another precaution set for safety then like going to the bathroom in groups is for women of today. Years ago when everybody knew everybody, things were a little different because there was already an established trace of who people were and how they could be found if something ever happened. Things are different today because some people are meeting each other in chat rooms where their real information is unverifiable and others are meeting people who have only come in to a town for a day or two and are never seen again. When I started dating, the dating process—in some ways—was much like applying for a job. Personal references were always necessary. We always had to know someone who could vouch for the young man that we liked. Someone who knew him before we did and could verify whether or not he was really a lunatic or had any crazy tendencies that we needed to know about before we got too close to him. Once my little sisters started dating, it was pretty normal for people to go on *blind dates*; and when they went on them and I could not be there to meet the young man, I would always tell them to call me as they were walking with their date to the car so that he could hear them tell me his name, what kind of car he was driving, and his license plate number out loud just so that he understood that even from a distance, someone was looking out for her well-being. Making sure that someone knew where we were going seemed to have come from the dating process but stuck with us even after. I remember visiting my mother one day after I had moved out of her home and thought that I was just grown enough to travel alone without telling anyone where I was going. In a casual conversation, I mentioned that I would be out of town and unreachable for a few days. After she asked me where I was going, I kind of played it to the side and said, I'll just be gone and told her that I would call her when I got back. She stopped me in my tracks and basically said, "Little girl, you don't have to tell me where you are going, but you need to tell someone in case you come up missing." That conversation readjusted my way of thinking about the subject and made me look out for my own safety in a different way.

The lessons that we learned about dating taught us to respect ourselves and helped us to be a great example to our date on how to respect us.

AN IMPORTANT PIECE: LEARNING ABOUT THE DATING PROCESS

There was never a time when our parents considered it to be okay for them to see us outside wrapped up, hugging or kissing some young man. They figured that that type of behavior should only be done inside of a house, and seeing as though we weren't old enough to have our own house, we pretty much had no business being in those positions at all. I can remember being a witness to my mother driving down the street past people who were all over one another outside and her saying things like "They need to go inside with that" or she would just outright warn us by saying, "I had better not ever see you outside disrespecting yourself like that or you will deeply regret it." From her reaction, we learned to know better. But in all fairness to truth, a lot of kids did these things outside because they could not do it in their parents' home. However, today there are parents who say, "Well, if my child is going to do certain things, I would rather it be done in my home so that I can keep an eye out on what is going on." But does it really make a difference if parents are sitting and watching their child do certain things that may not be the best decisions for their life in the long run? That way of thinking is okay when applying it to the dating process as a whole but not every detail of it to the extreme. We were expected to respect ourselves and to teach other people to respect us.

This taught us that there is a time and place for everything. We learned to have a certain class about ourselves.

AN IMPORTANT PIECE: DISPLAYING APPROPRIATE AFFECTION

Running up and leaning into a friend's or boyfriend's car when they pulled over to the side of the street to talk to us was another hot topic of discussion. Because it was something that prostitutes do as men drive their cars up to hire them for the evening, we were not allowed to do the same thing. When someone wanted to talk to us, they were expected to get out of their car and sit with us on the porch, in the house, or any other place that was considered to be respectable; and it didn't seem to bother my mom if someone didn't understand or appreciate her viewpoints as they pertained to our lives. Although she came across as being very soft-spoken, she always spoke her mind. She taught us that respect from others comes from respecting ourselves and that people will usually draw our portrait according to the pose we give them.

This lesson taught us to be aware of our self-image. Although we weren't brought up to be overly concerned about what other people thought, we were taught to carry ourselves in a respectable manner.

AN IMPORTANT PIECE: BEING AWARE OF AND RESPECTING OUR OWN IMAGE

We were taught through firsthand experience how to do certain things in life like properly keep a house clean, knowing how to cook, grocery shop, and manage the household finances. It was a *class* so to speak that we had to pass before moving out on our own. These were skills that grew to be an everyday part of life. After seeing people's different styles of cleaning during my college years, I was reminded of how my mom used to make me clean the bathroom. I couldn't just clean the sink and the mirror—which I personally thought was the fun part—but had to sweep then mop the floor and clean the tub and the toilet (cleaning the toilet was the worst). There was no *halfway* job to be done with anything because once I was finished, my mom would come and check my work. I thought it was so gross that I had to be so thorough and clean the ring around the water in the toilet, raise both lids, and then clean the ring around the top of the toilet too! Yuck! But I was shocked to learn that some kids had never been taught how to properly clean a toilet because someone else always did it for them. Our parents made us stretch our common sense to the fullest. They would say things like "That cleaner is not going to kill you unless you drink it, so make sure you don't drink it and just do what you are supposed to be doing." This made us as kids say things to each other like "Girl, I wouldn't put that stuff next to my mouth because that stuff will kill you." From cleaning to paying bills, we learned basic life skills. We were taught to always count our own money, sign our own checks, and that no one could ever lie to us about a truth that we knew firsthand to be fact. People years ago often figured that it was a waste of money to pay someone to do the things that you could do for yourself for free except at times when you were just not available to do to so. Handling our business was always a priority, and maintaining a household meant being able to run the business side of the family's business.

This prepared us to take care of our family's needs ourselves no matter what was going on around us. We were taught the skills to help us run a peaceful, productive household.

AN IMPORTANT PIECE: UNDERSTANDING HOW TO PROPERLY MAINTAIN A HOUSEHOLD

Although we were taught so many great points on what it meant to be a good mother, we were also taught that not everyone is meant to have their own children. We learned that everyone's purpose in life is different and that some people's life would include children and others' would not and that neither was a bad thing but just different. We were taught that regardless to what side of life that we found ourselves on, we were to be good-natured, loving, and understanding women toward every situation possible. However, if we decided that we wanted to have children, we needed to understand that there was a whole lot that would need to go into the process. Being a good mother meant sometimes taking the time to do things even when you don't "feel like it" when it is something that is important to your child. Doing things like playing with dolls, going to recitals, combing and cutting hair, cooking, cleaning, and having patience were just a few things on the list of trying to be a good mother. Making sacrifices was something else that was high on the list. Because my mom didn't let us go out with our friends when she was not at home because she wanted to be available for us if there was an emergency, she made the sacrifice when I was in middle school to quit her outside job and start a family day care so that she could be home for us when we needed her. Before she started this day care center, it was hard for me to see the parenting skills that she used to help us develop; but when I saw the things she did for the daycare children and how they affected their lives and then remembered that she had done those same things for us, it made me appreciate her more. She taught us to be caring to each other and even planted seeds in to the little girls' minds at the daycare about how they were supposed to always treat their baby dolls kindly. Whenever one of them threw their dolls around, she'd walk up to them and say in a very calm voice, "Oh no. Is that how you treat your baby?" as she would then pick the doll up and rub its head and ask them, "Now is that how people treat you? You have to be kind and gentle to your baby. You have to treat it right and show it that you love it." The look on the children's faces was always such that they really understood her point. Regardless of whether or not we wanted to have our own children, we were taught to be kind to people around us.

The best lessons of how to be and what it meant to be a loving woman was from the example that was shown to us at home. We learned that it is not about the time that you have to connect with people, but it is about the moments that you have when you connect.

AN IMPORTANT PIECE: BEING LOVING TOWARD OTHERS

CHAPTER SEVEN

Family Ties

Family Ties

This chapter mirrors many of the circumstances and experiences that tied families together through the good and the bad times in life.

TIED TOGETHER BY:

Good parenting

Big Mama, Granny and Madea

Balanced time

What family time used to be

Summer vacations

Understanding the concept of siblings vs. friends

The work to live versus the live to work mentality

Investing into children

Taking care of one another

Christmas time not Christmas gifts

The little things in life

Sunday's rituals

Church-The Family Tie

SEVEN

My mother and many from her generation understood that whoever is a child's primary caregiver; feeding them, taking care of them when they are sick, helping them with their homework, and is involved with events like school conferences or extracurricular activities on a regular basis, be it the parent, grandparent, or nanny will more than likely been seen in the eyes of the child as their parent. They may not hold the title verbally, but it is often held in the heart of the child. A lot of us, just like the generations in the past want to be good parents and spend as much time with our children as we can but because of our workloads, it is almost seems impossible at times. Even though my mom worked a lot, she tried to implement those "mommy and me" moments as much as possible. I have found that most children do not remember every moment spent, instead, they remember moments as if they were snapshots captured through photos. I've often said that with children, it's not always about the time spent but the memories captured. I'd rather my daughters say that although I didn't always have all the time that they would have liked for me to be able to spend with them, the memories that we shared together were so full that they were able to fill their hearts with those moments of joy.

Even though at times we had babysitters, we learned—based on the active role that my mother took with us—that she took pride in filling the responsibility as our parent; and although we had great relationships with other people in our lives, no one would ever take her place. We learned through her doings what it meant to be a good parent.

TIED TOGETHER BY GOOD PARENTING

There were once three words when we heard them as children made us feel warm, safe, and our stomachs full; they were *big—mama*, *madea* (short for *mother dear*), and *granny*. These were the names set aside for grandmothers, who always made sure that every child was taken care of. They made sure that we all had warm blankets even if it meant that they had to make them by hand. My favorite blankets as a kid were those that they handmade by gathering a lot of blankets and encasing them between two nice pieces of fabric. They were so heavy and warm and always reminded me of someone's grandmother because they seemed to be the only people who knew how to make them. Grandmothers always made us feel safe because they were constantly telling us that they would never let anything happened to us. Our stomachs were always full because it seemed that at all times there was a hot plate of food on their table waiting for us to arrive. My great-aunt served as an additional grandmother to me and we seemed to have so much fun together. It may have had to do with the fact that she was always full of treats and snacks and all that I wanted as a child. We'd go on grocery store runs and little trips together that were always full of fun. Those were the days. When I was younger, my Big Mama was my great-grandmother. Everyone in the family knew who she was because she had over ten children who also had a lot of children and she was known and looked to as the beginning of our immediate family. The words *big mama* and *madea* were titles that at one point were considered to be given to the ultimate grandmother. Because people gathered at her house on a regular basis there was no real need for a traditional family reunion every year. Today there are so many grandmothers who will not even allow their grandchildren to call them grandma, grand-mama, or anything that might send a sign to the public that she is old enough to have grandchildren. Some of these women are the thirty-something-year-old single grandmothers who, although they had their children when they were teenagers, just like Big Mama and Madea may have chosen to relive the years they felt like they gave up to raise their children. By the time their children started having children of their own and may have needed a little help, the thought of them not having the last of their "young years" to themselves was not an option. At that point, many are ready to date again, settle down, and possibly even have more children with their new husbands. These women make it very clear that they will not be babysitting their grandchildren because it might interrupt their dating schedules and social lives. They are more concerned about being perceived as young, vibrant women in the dating world rather than as someone's grandmother. Years ago, when a young woman had a child, her family pushed her to the realization that she was no longer a single woman free of responsibility. Of course, there were always exceptions. However, many realized that they were going to be a mother; and whether they liked it or not, they would have to attend to their children's needs. Today's "Missing Grandmothers Society" seems to have some of the same issues with accepting that they are grandmothers and are in need of being pushed to accept their role as such.

We learned that just as our mother holds a special place and memory in our lives, our grandmother has her own special place as well. For us, she represented a soft place for us to lay our head, a love that was unconditional and not judgmental, and someone who had the ability to see past our problems and straight to our hearts.

TIED TOGETHER BY BIG MAMA, GRANNY AND MADEA

Due to the fact that there are only so many hours in a day and most people these days have to work, family time can be hard to plan. By the end of a long day at work, it's normal to sometimes feel that picking up the kids, feeding them, checking their homework, and putting them to bed should just be enough. For me, trying to squeeze time in with the family and have a little time for myself sometimes seems impossible. Back in the day, there were real support systems available to parents who needed a little "me-time." These systems were built from teams of mothers, aunts, sisters, friends, and even neighbors who would step in and offer to watch someone's children when they needed to take a moment of time-out for themselves. This type of support allowed parents to calm down from problems that may have happened throughout the day. People would say to each other, "Bring your kids over my house, and let them play in the back room with my kids while we make a nice dinner and just talk." Unfortunately, today there is not the same kind of help being offered like there used to be. Because a lot of parents have to do everything on their own, they sometimes feel forced to take "emergency time-outs" that emerge right before mental breakdowns. It can be especially difficult for single parents who often try so hard to make life feel as though "everything is normal" for their children even though the other parent may not be around. The parents from our day realized that if they took the time to explain to us that they couldn't do everything by themselves and that we might have to make some adjustments in our lives, they wouldn't have the added stress of worrying about how we were feeling and whether or not our lives were normal. They also reminded us that a "normal lifestyle" is relative to our situation and that we should not get caught up in how it may seem that we are different from others. Otherwise, it becomes too exhausting and people begin to breakdown before they realize that they cannot do everything by themselves or on everyone's life schedule. There are also those who live in a "me first" phase of life and feel that it is just too much of a sacrifice to make certain lifestyle adjustments in their lives for the benefit of their children. Instead of carving out family time for their kids, they make their children find family time somewhere within their social lives and take them to parties and events that are not age appropriate but because they want to go and feel that they should spend some time with their kids, they take the kids along for the ride. Because of the lack of support systems and the "me first" mentality these days, some parents decide that they really just want to have a life of their own and that their children just have to fall in line with their lifestyle.

We were taught that there can still be a balance on the scale of life even though the weight might change on one side, giving priorities to certain aspects.

TIED TOGETHER BY BALANCED TIME

"Family time" was once a commonly used expression. We looked forward to having as much time together as we could get.

Spending time together in those days was different than it is today because money was limited and families were larger. Kids weren't allowed to have such high expectations on what they wanted to do but appreciated whatever plans were made. Sunday dinners were often a time to "sit down, take a look at each other, and enjoy the essence of what we had at that moment." It was much easier for families to find the time to spend together in those days because there weren't as many options to do other things like there are today. The amount of time that we had was guided by our parents' schedule who oftentimes went to work and then came right home. The fact that most people had a lot less money to spend on frivolous things made them take the time to focus on the things that were the most important like their families. When we got together, the focus was not as much about the plan for the day as much as it was about who was going to be there to spend time together. Back then time spent would often be as simple as children playing together in the back room of a house or in the yard while the adults just sat and talked to each other while playing cards or dominos in the living room. It was something that we looked forward to. Going over to one of our aunts', uncles', or grandparents' houses, or the fact that our cousins were coming to our house, gave us something to look forward to and made us happy. Our family instilled in us, through these times, a love for family. Our parents were very resourceful in everything that they did for us. When we were able to go to amusement parks, we were super excited. It was never about how many things we could buy when we got there but about the fact that we were getting to go. We didn't look forward to eating the expensive food that was sold at the park because our mom, aunts, and cousins usually prepared food for us to take with us. They'd pack sandwiches, chicken, a few side dishes, and even slide drinks in a backpack for us to enjoy while we were there. Where ever we went, we always packed food. I remember the memories of going to the drive-in movies with a backpack full of sandwiches, popcorn, and snacks. We were so excited to be at the movies . . . having homemade food was an *extra* that we would have been just as happy and appreciative without. Our parents figured out activities that we could do together. We didn't have it like some kids do today where their parents give each child some money individually and say, "Hey, go call one of your friends and figure out what you are going to do today." During the times when our parents decided to treat us and give us a set amount of money, it was usually to be spent for us as a group of siblings or even cousins. Whether or not we decided to go to the movies or the mall, we learned to negotiate with each other to figure something out that made us all happy. If someone got upset because they didn't get a chance to do what they wanted to do, they were quickly reminded that they didn't have to go in the first place if they couldn't figure out how to appreciate the opportunity that had been given to them. There were also many times when our parents took whatever money they might have given to us to go out and instead bought something fun for us to do together at home. We also spent a lot of family time traveling together, but it was viewed much differently then than it is today. Going by car was the most common way to travel because many people didn't like to fly, and some of those who did, didn't have the money to buy one plane ticket let alone plane tickets for the entire family. Because the point of going on the trip was to spend time together, our parents had to find a way that worked for everyone. Today, fewer families travel together with their entire family. We live in such an instant society where patience is hard to find and people do not want to be in the car together for a long period time, so they prefer to fly. Unfortunately, because it is still too expensive today for most to buy plane tickets for their entire family and still pay for other necessary accommodations, parents often travel together and leave their children behind. I never felt like my mother ever considered leaving us behind unless we were being sent somewhere to spend time with other family members for the summertime. It was so normal for us to pack up the car and hit the highway. It wasn't always the most comfortable situation to be in; but it forced us to bond in a way that, at the time, may not have been appreciated but—looking back on it—was a great thing. Those road trips taught us to practice patience. Traveling across country as a family also allowed us to see places and have experiences that we would not have been able to afford to see otherwise. It was not only how we had to travel but was also something that we looked forward to doing. The time that we spent together as a family taught us that, unlike today, it was more about the time spent together (quality versus quantity) than anything else. We also learned how to enjoy each other's company. There are some families who refuse to spend time together unless there is an activity or distraction planned that takes the focus off of them actually having to talk to each other and spend real quality time together. Some husbands and wives can *make it* as long as they have enough money to travel together or are even able to take separate vacations.

We learned that we had to get along with each other because we were—most of the time—all we had, and everything else that we got was extra. Even as our family acquired more, we were reminded that we didn't have to have anything and to make the best of what we had.

TIED TOGETHER BY WHAT FAMILY TIME USED TO BE

Our summer vacations were a well-awaited time of the year that we so looked forward to. We not only grew in size over the summer months but seemed to learn so much over the break that grew our minds through our experiences. By the time it was the end of each school year, we usually knew of at least one place that we were going to visit during our summer vacation. Many of us spent quite a few summer vacations visiting with our family members who lived a long distance away. It was once a common practice for parents to send their children to visit with their grandparents, aunts, uncles, and cousins that they didn't get a lot of time to see during the rest of the year for at least a couple of weeks and sometimes a couple of months during the summertime. As people moved from one part of the country to another, it became more and more important for their children's feet to touch the grounds where their family had traveled from. We experienced a part of our family's roots in our parents' attempt to help us better understand ourselves. During those times, we did things that we never had the opportunity or need to do while living in the city. We picked wild berries for our aunts who then used them to bake cobblers, peaches from the trees just to have a snack and experienced dirt roads and ditches made from clay. Because we weren't allowed to run in and out of the house, we learned how to rinse fruit off with the water hose outside and be satisfied. Today, many of us find it hard to send or take our kids to places that our parents came from, even though we remember the lessons that we learned by just being there. When we were not visiting distant relatives during the summer, we were on road trips with our immediate families or spending time with family members who lived nearby while our parents were at work.

Going back to where our immediate family originated helped us to gain a sense of self and better understanding of our history. We learned that spending time with family was sometimes a mirrored experience that helped us to see the reflection of ourselves within our family. Seeing the good or bad allowed us to decide whether or not we wanted to continue to do those things that we saw them do or make certain changes. Being around family also helped us to understand that we are not alone in this world.

TIED TOGETHER BY SUMMER VACATIONS

Although my friends were very special to me and some have been a part of my life now for over twenty years I was raised to understand that my best friends were my siblings. Growing up, we had our fair share of arguments and fights like everyone else but were reminded to be kind to each other because at the end of the day, all we might have is each other. I wish I had understood that better as a child. We were reminded that we knew each other better than anyone else around and therefore could sometimes give the best advice about whatever the other person was going through. Over time, I was able to see that that my friends wanted to do everything with me that my sister already did with me on an everyday basis. Things like having sleepovers, going to the mall or the grocery store together, having dinner and going on family trips were all the things that we begged our parents to let us do with our friends but were able to do with our siblings all the time. My parents realized that my friends were an important part of my development. However, the reality was that there were only so many hours in a day to be with them. I was allowed to play with them at school and after school if they lived in my neighborhood, but my parents made it very clear that they were not going to be run by my social schedule. I remember asking my mother if I could play with my school friends on the weekends. Her response was, "Didn't you play with those kids all week at school?" Now that I have kids, I see how funny and true that statement really is. The friends that we played with on most weekends were either related to us, lived in the neighborhood, or were the children of our parent's friends. Although we didn't really get to hang out at all of our friend's homes, we were allowed to play with our parents' friends' children at their homes because our parents knew their parents and felt comfortable with not only the children, but also with the parents, and were familiar with their family as a whole. They often seemed more like our extended families because on many occasions, our parents would be at their house while we played. When my children were younger, they were involved in quite a few programs. I wasn't familiar with the social schedules that many children have today. I thought it was so sweet that the mothers in these programs would be so kind to offer to pick my children up and take them to their homes to play, but I wanted to get to know these families first. I was used to getting to know someone's family, getting comfortable in their household, and then taking my child to their house to play if I had time in my schedule to do so. Scheduling dates to play every weekend and after school for the sake of my child's social life was new to me. I remember my mother saying to me, "You are not going to run me," which was short for, "You are not going to run me crazy or ragged running you all over town especially when it's not necessary." The weekend was our time to hang out and bond with our family. Do not get me wrong; some of the parents of my children's friends have become several of my close friends. However, those bonds were bound together by the relationship that the parent and I created after getting to know each other first. I've often been teased about being too protective of my daughters, but when I send my children to hang out at someone's home, it is important that I get to know my child's friend, their parents, as well as be familiar with anyone else that lives in the home. It only takes one time for something to happen that may ruin or change their lives forever. It is certainly true that bad things can happen with people that we would never expect, but as a parent, I would hate to feel that I didn't do my job of checking out my child's environment in hopes of keeping them safe.

It wasn't until my sisters and I were older that we realized how special it is to have a tight bond with your siblings. Although we shared a bond that at times may have seemed strained, once we understood that we are not only siblings but also lifelong friends, it helped to put things into perspective. Our parents taught us that although it is important to value your outside friendships, it is more important to value friendships with your family.

TIED TOGETHER BY UNDERSTANDING THE CONCEPT OF SIBLINGS VERSUS FRIENDS

For many people today, going to work is viewed differently than it was years ago. People used to use the phrase "going off to work" when they went to work each day because they felt the pressure of leaving their families and homes to go and work. The only enjoyment that came from a hard day's work was the fact that they knew that their family would be provided for based on their labor. However, today, many people do not work to live but live to work. They are motivated to think this way because either their job is so much fun that they value it more than their family or they value material possessions (e.g., bigger homes, nicer cars, etc.) more than their family. The big picture of life gets lost as quality time with family is traded in for possessions. "Keeping up with the Joneses" was a phrase once used as some people began to earn more money. Although everyone's pay did not increase, many people still felt the need to appear as though they were able to keep up with everyone else. This created a horrible cycle where people began spending more money than they earned. Due to this problem, it became necessary for them to work longer hours in an effort to make more money and appear to be on top. I taught my children early on, based on my own experiences that *they can have anything, but they can't have everything.*" This may sound harsh, but it simply means that priorities have to be set in life. People cannot work 80-120 hours a week and expect to know about everything that is going on within their families' day-to-day life. Some thing will be missed. This is why it is so important to set priorities and, if nothing else, decide what facts about your family's day that you have to be in the know about. Choose some way to stay connected to them on a daily basis. Growing up, I always felt that my mother was connected to me even when she was at working.

We learned to not get so caught up in what we do professionally that we miss who and why we are doing it.

TIED TOGETHER BY THE WORK TO LIVE VERSUS LIVE TO WORK MENTALITY

As children, we did not know anything about what investments were or realize how our parents were investing so much of themselves and their time and effort in us. What we realized over time was that they cared so much about us that they were invested in every part of our lives. As adults, we understood the value of having parents who took the time to invest in who we needed to be as adults. We felt the love that came from their hearts and appreciated the time that was spent in disciplining us out of that love in an effort to give us a better understanding of life. As we grew up, we saw firsthand families that did not spend time with their children and how it affected their children's lives. Because my mother invested so much in us when we couldn't take care of ourselves, it made us realize that it would only be right for us to take care of her when she gets to a point where she can no longer take care of herself. As a parent, I know how exhausting it can be to devote so much time to a child. It can almost be overwhelming at times to stay focused on the long-term goal. I hear people say that it's better or easier to just let children develop on their own, allowing them to be free to be whoever they are going to be. It may be easier in the beginning but certainly not in the end. A child is like a clay mold that is soft in the beginning and has the ability to be shaped. As they start to dry, or get older, they harden into whatever they were molded into or however they were allowed to fall into place. It is then possible but very hard to reshape who they are once they're dry without cracking them, but is easier to go through the process of taking the time to mold them correctly when they're young.

We learned from watching how our parents invested in to us and then seeing the outcome of people who didn't have anyone to

invest in to them that whatever is put into children when they are
young is what comes out of them when they are older.

TIED TOGETHER BY INVESTING INTO CHILDREN

It seems that more and more people are putting their parents in convalescent homes these days. That was unheard of when I was growing up. Parents spent so much time with their children and made so many sacrifices for them that to then put them in a convalescent home when they were in need of care did not seem right. Some people felt as though they owed it to their parents to care for them as much as they possibly could. Although many families didn't have the money to add on a guesthouse to accommodate their parents' needs, people made it work however they could. Any extra room in the house suited them just fine, and it sometimes meant that some of the children were made to share a room to create an extra room. If there was no extra room in any of the back bedrooms or den, the front room—also known as the living room—was used instead. It was once so common that it didn't seem strange to walk into someone's house and see a hospital bed in the living room. This may be a hard thing to do in families of today because this type of sacrifice requires that everyone in the household have a good understanding of what is best for the family. Although so many explanations are given to the children of today about so many different kinds of things, some parents do not want to take the time to explain to their children that they may have to give up their personal space to be of help to a family member. Strangely enough, this is often not because the child would not understand but because it makes the parent feel uncomfortable to have to do so. We understood this type of sacrifice as something that families did for one another when in need. Children are an investment. If you love and take care of them as they are growing up and are in need, in most cases, they will love and take care of you when you are in need.

We learned to take care of our family members.

TIED TOGETHER OF TAKING CARE OF ONE ANOTHER (CONVALESCENT HOMES VERSUS THE BACK ROOM)

We didn't have a lot of extra money around or credit cards to max out when I was little. My mom bought us the gifts that she could as we celebrated the Christmas holiday and taught us that the holiday was not about the gift exchange but about the *holy day* itself. Our memories from the holidays were based around the time that we spent with our family laughing and sharing a meal together more so than anything else. Most families, if nothing else, would make an effort to come together to share a wonderful Christmas dinner. Mothers started preparing for the meal a week before the dinner was scheduled. They would begin with the cakes, pies, and breads, and—as they got closer to the holiday—would prepare the main dishes. It was a time of family. We have fallen victim to today's marketing schemes that push us to believe that Christmas is only about the gifts given and received. A lot of children who celebrate the holiday are not even being given a background on what it is really about. They learn from the media that the *winner* is the person who receives the best gifts and spends the most money buying the most expensive gifts for others. Through this, they are being taught that it's okay to spend more than they can afford and that living in debt and beyond their means is okay as long as they look good in the eyes of others.

We learned that the Christmas holiday was not our birthday party but that we were celebrating Jesus' birthday and that when we go to a birthday party we might get to have fun and eat great food but that it is not about receiving gifts while we're there.

TIED TOGETHER BY CHRISTMAS TIME . . . NOT CHRISTMAS GIFTS

As my mom entered the door coming home from work, we would always ask her, "What did you bring us?" She would laugh and say, "Me. I brought you me." But on the Fridays that she got paid, she would try to have a little something extra for us. Be it a coloring book or a snack, we were excited and so happy that she thought about us. Unlike some kids of today, it never crossed our minds to ask how much something cost or ask for something expensive just because we knew it was expensive. When we wanted to have what we considered to be a fancy dinner, we didn't need to go to a fancy restaurant to have one. When my mom wanted us to feel like we were going to a restaurant, she would prepare a special meal that for us seemed as though it came right off a fancy menu. It is always confusing for me when I hear parents complain about all the expensive things that their children ask for, that they then turn around and buy. Some parents say, "It's just too hard to tell them no. It's easier to just give them what they want." However, when the situation is handled this way, the child never learns how to appreciate what is given to them and, oftentimes, continues to ask for more while learning that their parents don't mean what they say. Our parents made a big deal out of the little things that were given to us when we were young, which helped to train our perception on how much it really took to be a big deal in our eyes of appreciation. Although we were raised to be grounded, we still occasionally asked for the things that our friends had. We may have even come to our parents a few times with a few requests, but because they took the time to teach us the logic behind certain answers, we learned to think about our questions all the way through before we asked them. This, in many cases, caused our parents to respect our questions more, knowing that they took the time to think them through before we came to them—which seemed to make them want to do more for us and, in turn, encouraged us to continue to make the right choices.

The fact that appreciation mostly comes from not having taught us to really appreciate the little things that our parents were able to bring us when they got paid or had a little extra money.

TIED TOGETHER BY THE LITTLE THINGS IN LIFE

In our house, we recognized Sunday as "the LORD's Day" and celebrated it as so. There were very specific things that we were and were not allowed to do on that day. Because the Bible stated that the LORD took a day of rest, we were taught to do the same. There was no such thing as doing housework or running errands on Sunday. We had fun times with our friends over the weekend, but it was understood that everything that needed to be done over the weekend had to be done on Saturday. We hung out as late as we were allowed to on Saturday nights but always knew that, regardless to how late we stayed up, there was no falling asleep in church on Sunday morning or we were in big trouble. When we were caught nodding off in Sunday's service, we would be given the speech about how, if we couldn't stay awake in church, we must have stayed up too late the night before and our bedtime or curfew needed to be adjusted. If we could stay awake all night and do things with our friends, we were required to stay up during the church sermon. Sunday was reserved strictly for going to church, spending time with our family, and enjoying a nice Sunday dinner.

This was our introduction to setting priorities in life. Through these rituals, we learned that life is not only about our jobs and our friends but that God and then family come first.

TIED TOGETHER BY SUNDAY'S RITUALS

Church was not only a place to worship but also served the people of the community in so many ways. It was the place that everyone in the neighborhood went to for any kind of help. The principles taught there lined the roads of our lives and became our foundation. A lot of people referred to the members of the church as their "church family" because once someone was a member, they were looked after as family by the other members. It was also and is still a common place for an entire community to meet and talk about the changes happening in the world. Pastors address the issues of the times and people gravitate there as a place of refuge. People gather to pray about life's issues, talk about the things that are going on in the community, and listen to the choir sing the song for the day. The choir's songs have been and continue to be the soundtrack of many of our lives. The songs sung on a Sunday literally help motivate people throughout the entire week. When going through difficult times, the words of the songs that the choir sang on Sunday are often the encouragement needed to push someone through their day. The community within the church helped us as children to learn that there is more to life than our own interests. It also gave children as well as adults a sense of security and stability, especially for those whose homes were not a stable environment. It is often the bridge of hope toward the

faith needed for families during their time of need. There are still
many great churches that serve the same purpose today. There is
so much talk these days about how there aren't free after-school
programs for children and young adults anymore and how bored
children are because they have nothing to do. For many children,
church was definitely the number one after-school program.
We were expected to not only do our homework and chores but
to also know what was going on at any given night. Be it choir
rehearsal, Bible study, prayer services, helping to fold napkins for
a banquet, or folding programs for Sunday morning service, there
was always something to do at the church. This is what helped
keep many children that would have otherwise been wandering
around the neighborhood focused on the right track, out of trouble,
and understanding that someone was paying attention to him or
her. If our parents couldn't make it to church, they would send us
with one of the "church mothers" who were happy to have us help
them work on a project with them rather than having us somewhere
else. Church mothers were a gift to us all. Although there are still
many active church mothers, their presence is not felt as much
as it used to be. These are the women that are not just members
of the church but are a part of the village that help to keep the
church and community functioning as a whole and practically live
there. We would always know who they were because they were
referred to as *Mother* Johnson or *Mother* Harris because of the
role that they took on. Years ago, church mothers were the women
who were the community welcoming committee to families who
were in need. In those days, when people moved to a new city,
they not only looked for a new home for their families but also
for a new church home. Many people looked at the church as the
heart of their foundation and the go-to place for everything that
happened in their community. The experience that they had when
they visited a church was very important. The church mothers
would pay close attention to the new families and greet them as
they walked up and came in. They would find out where each
family was from and if they needed anything. People could go
to them for help if his or her electricity was being shut off. If
they needed food, the *mothers* would find out how many people
lived in their household and see to it that a box of food was sent
to their home right away. People worked hard to provide for their

families, but when they were not able to do so, many did not let their pride get in the way of them asking for help and were very appreciative of anything that was given to them. Today there are people who, although they may not be able afford to buy their own groceries, do not want to ask for help or accept generic brand items offered to them because of their pride. The church mothers introduced the new members to old members in an attempt to make them feel more comfortable. We were taught that people are to come to church as they are, even when it came to what they were wearing. If a woman came to church in a low-cut top or a really short skirt, church mothers—without placing judgment—would discreetly pull her to the side and explain to her that her lack of clothing might be a distraction from the Word of God that was being taught and would offer to provide her with additional clothing. If a man walked in with clothes or shoes that were torn and appeared to need help, they would offer to provide for him and meet his needs as well. A family's needs did not get ignored. People knew that they could go to the *mother's* board of directors, ask for help, and feel confident that anything and everything would be done to make sure they were taken care of without being judged. These women were amazing to watch. They also cooked for and coordinated every church and other community events. Whether it was the Christmas program, the pastor's anniversary dinner, or a fund-raiser, the church mothers were always the official coordinators. They would organize, cook, handle the preparations, and clean up after the event so that everyone else could enjoy themselves.

This type of fellowship showed us that no matter what is going on in the world, we can always come together in our community to not only talk about problems, but to also pray about them as well. Because our parents made sure that we participated in activities that taught us about responsibility, getting to know our neighbors, being a part of a community, and other things that tapped into our spirits and reminded us that there was a bigger purpose in life aside from the things that we wanted, we grew to understand that our life's purpose was bigger than we thought. We were sent not only to serve but also to receive certain values that were deposited in to who we were to become as adults. Church mothers helped to remind us how important it is to have the help of a village. These women step up to the plate and become a mother and true support system to so many people in need.

TIED TOGETHER BY CHURCH The Family Tie . . .

The greatness of the country that we have grown to know and love was built on the values, practices, and lessons that were taught to many generations of children that helped us all push farther in life in a positive direction. Our country will continue to push forward in the direction in which we raise the next generation of children.

INDEX

SAYINGS USED:

PATIENCE LEARNED THROUGH:

GUIDANCE TAUGHT THROUGH:

LaVergne, TN USA
30 September 2009
159515LV00001B/266/P